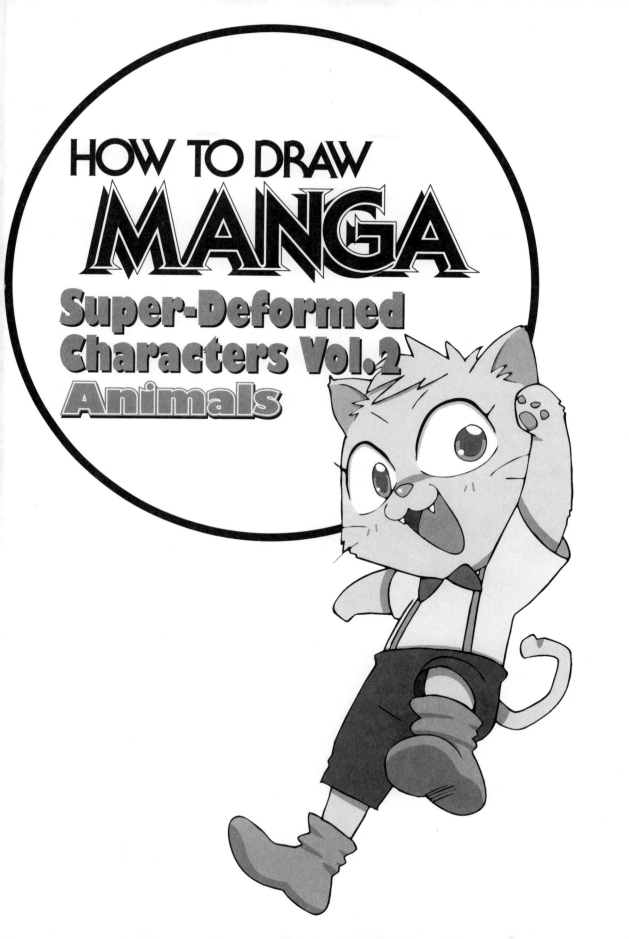

HOW TO DRAW MANGA
Super-Deformed Characters Vol. 2
Animals

HOW TO DRAW MANGA: Super-Deformed Characters Vol. 2
Animals
by Gen Sato

Copyright © 2004 Gen Sato
Copyright © 2004 Graphic-sha Publishing Co., Ltd.

This book was first designed and produced by Graphic-sha Publishing Co., Ltd.
in Japan in 2004. This English edition was published by Graphic-sha Publishing Co., Ltd.
in Japan in 2005.

Graphic-sha Publishing Co., Ltd.
1-14-17 Kudan-kita, Chiyoda-ku, Tokyo 102-0073 Japan

Cover Illustration:	Gen Sato
Book Illustrations:	Gen Sato, Asami Ogasawara. Yasuhito Irie, Miyako Kubo
Original Book Design:	Miho Kato (tap)
Main title Logo Design:	Hideyuki Amemura
Planning Editor:	Kuniyoshi Masujima (Graphic-sha Publishing Co., Ltd.)
English Edition Layout:	Shinichi Ishioka
English Translation Management:	Língua fránca, Inc. (an3y-skmt@asahi-net.or.jp)

Foreign Language Edition Project Coordinator: Kumiko Sakamoto (Graphic-sha Publishing Co., Ltd.)

Distributed by
Japanime Co., Ltd.
3-31-18 Nishi-kawaguchi, Kawaguchi-shi,
Saitama 332-0021, Japan
Phone/Fax: +81-(0)48-259-3444
E-mail: sales@japanime.com
http://www.japanime.com

First printing: June 2005

ISBN: 4-7661-1470-1
Printed and bound in China by Everbest Printing Co., Ltd.

Table of Contents

Foreword 4

Chapter 1
Chibi Animals as Basic Geometric Shapes.... 5
These are all the shapes you'll need!........................ 6
Circle, Square, Trapezoid, Triangle, Ellipse,
Gourd-Shape, Rectangle, Semicircles

Chapter 2
Turning Animals into Super-Deformed Characters 19
Dogs 20
Cats 24
Hamsters 30
Rabbits 32
Squirrels and Chipmunks 33
Prairie Dogs 35
Mice 36
Monkeys 37
Foxes 38
Raccoon Dogs 39
Seals and Hedgehogs 40
Koalas and Otters 42
Horses 43
Cows and Bulls 46
Sheep 47
Donkeys 48
Pigs 50
Boars 51
Goats 52
Lions 53
Tigers 54
Elephants 56
Rhinoceroses 58
Hippopotamuses 59
Camels 60
Giraffes 61
Gorillas 62
Pandas 63
Bears 64
Wolves 68
Kangaroos 69
Owls 71
Cranes, Sparrows, and Swallows 72
Swans 73
Crows 74
Eagles and Hawks 75
Ducks and Geese 76

Chickens 78
Peacocks 79
Porpoises 81
Whales and Orcas 82
Penguins 84
Tuna and Sharks 85
Octopuses 86
Squids 87
Mollusks 88
Shrimp and Jellyfish 90
Snakes 94
Frogs 95
Iguanas 97
Geckos and Salamanders 98
Turtles 99
Chameleons 100
Bats and Grasshoppers 101
Beetles, Scorpions, and Cockroaches 102
Dragons 103
Dinosaurs 105
Unicorns, Pegasus, and the Phoenix 107

Chapter 3
Things Can Be Chibis Too! 115
Ultra-Stylized Objects 116
Bowls and TV Sets 118
Knives and Drums 119
Buckets and Mechanical Pencils 120
Irons and Geta 121
Cigarettes, Fans, and Brushes 122
Batteries, Lipstick, and Balloons 123
Dishes and Newspapers 124
Chairs, Couches, and Soap 125
Afterword & about the author 126

Column: Q&A
What is anthropomorphism? 17
Q&A 1 28
Q&A 2 29
Q&A 3 41
Q&A 4 66
Q&A 5 67
Q&A 6 70
Q&A 7 80
Q&A 8 92
Q&A 9 93
Q&A 10 109
Game Illustration Gallery 110

Animals and objects are fun to chibify too!

We have compiled this volume on ultra-stylized animals as a follow up to our popular volume *How to Draw Super-Deformed Characters Volume 1: Humans.* As discussed in the previous book, again we stress that the most important element to drawing chibi characters is developing a consistent milieu or world for the character to inhabit.

Even if you have rendered your chibi character to perfection, if the background is awkwardly realistic or if the props surrounding your character are all drawn in a naturalized style, then your beautifully drawn chibi's appeal will be lost among its surroundings. Settings that bring chibi characters to life require consistency in their construction. Consequently to achieve these ends, the artist needs to apply the ultra-stylization techniques learned in Volume 1 to all the components of the chibi's world. In this book, we focus on animals and objects that appear in the vast world of chibi characters.

As the reader is likely aware, we, as people, live close to many animals and even have made them our friends. There are people who have achieved communication of sorts with animals, and more than a few animal lovers who have come to understand their feelings quite well.

Like people, animals display emotions and individual personalities. In other words, they possess many qualities that make them suitable chibi characters, and if you, the artist, are able to identify these key qualities, you should find it relatively easy to create appealing chibi characters.

Many readers may harbor some doubts regarding chibi objects. In the preceding paragraphs and in the first volume, we stressed emotions and personality as key elements in creating ultra-stylized, super-deformed characters. However, if you are to achieve a uniform chibi world, then objects must undergo ultra-stylization as well.

Thus, in this book we will attempt two modes of chibi-zation. While this might seem a bit difficult to some readers, I assure you that I am still trying to master techniques in creating chibi characters myself, so this is a subject we will explore together.

Chapter 1

Chibi Animals as Basic Geometric Shapes

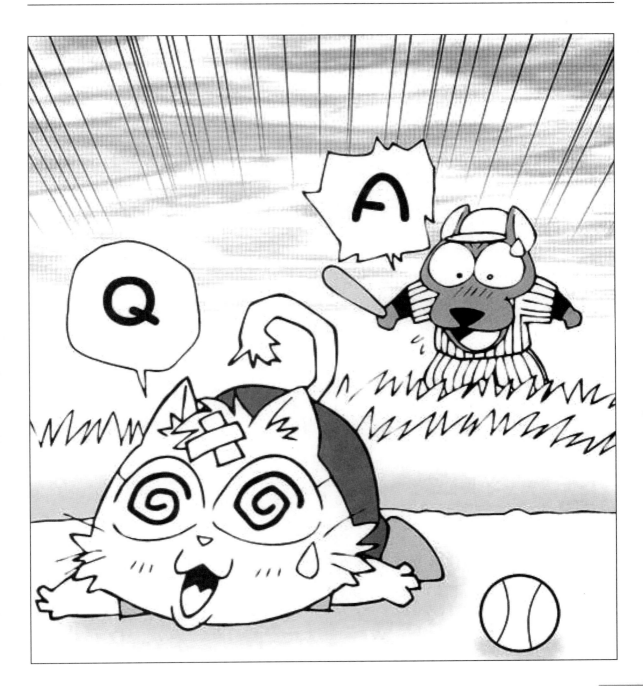

These are all the shapes you'll need!

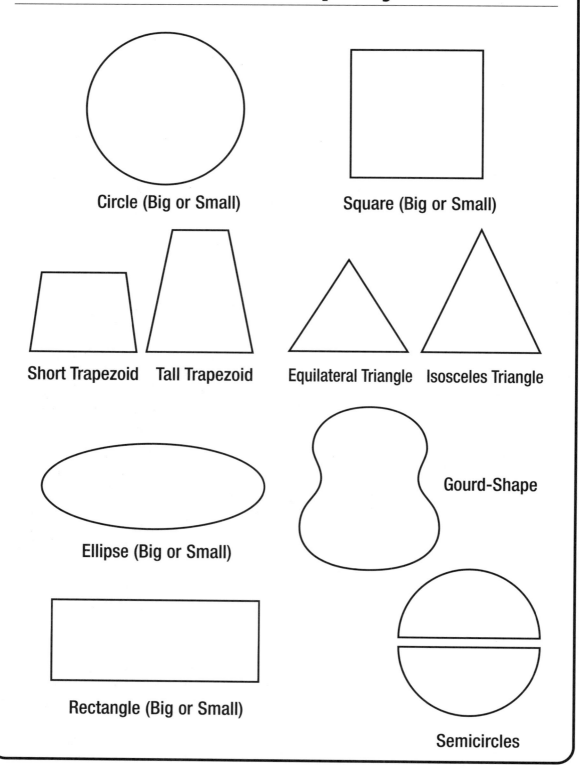

Circle (Big or Small)

Square (Big or Small)

Short Trapezoid   Tall Trapezoid

Equilateral Triangle   Isosceles Triangle

Ellipse (Big or Small)

Gourd-Shape

Rectangle (Big or Small)

Semicircles

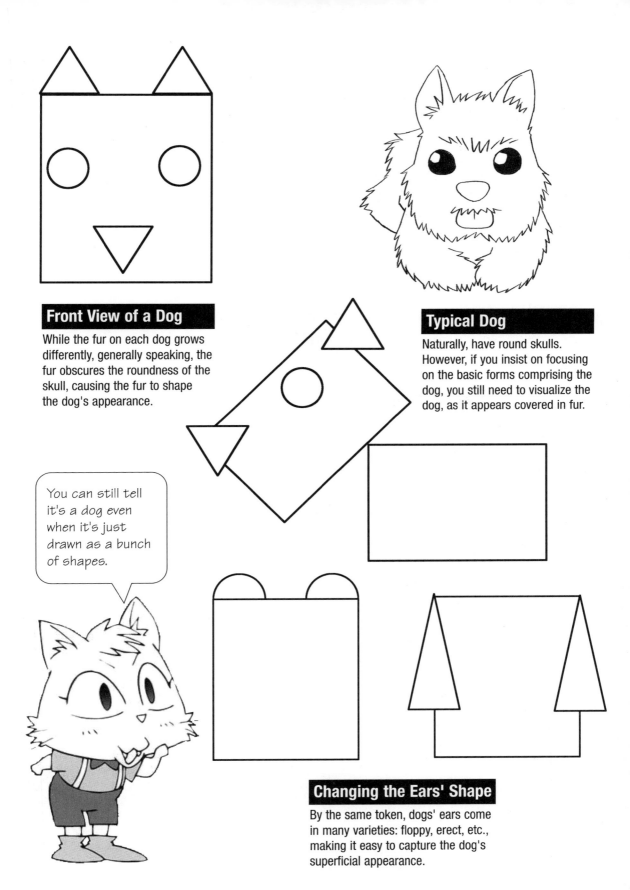

Front View of a Dog

While the fur on each dog grows differently, generally speaking, the fur obscures the roundness of the skull, causing the fur to shape the dog's appearance.

Typical Dog

Naturally, have round skulls. However, if you insist on focusing on the basic forms comprising the dog, you still need to visualize the dog, as it appears covered in fur.

You can still tell it's a dog even when it's just drawn as a bunch of shapes.

Changing the Ears' Shape

By the same token, dogs' ears come in many varieties: floppy, erect, etc., making it easy to capture the dog's superficial appearance.

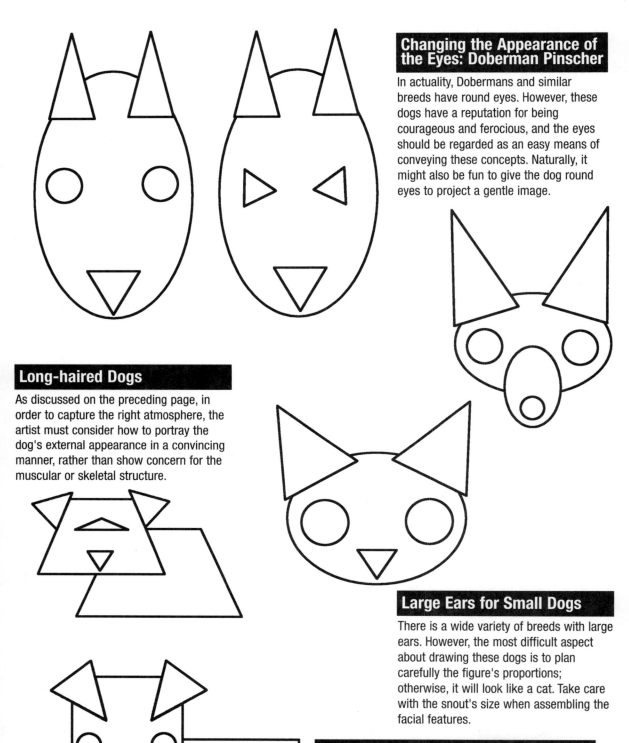

Changing the Appearance of the Eyes: Doberman Pinscher

In actuality, Dobermans and similar breeds have round eyes. However, these dogs have a reputation for being courageous and ferocious, and the eyes should be regarded as an easy means of conveying these concepts. Naturally, it might also be fun to give the dog round eyes to project a gentle image.

Long-haired Dogs

As discussed on the preceding page, in order to capture the right atmosphere, the artist must consider how to portray the dog's external appearance in a convincing manner, rather than show concern for the muscular or skeletal structure.

Large Ears for Small Dogs

There is a wide variety of breeds with large ears. However, the most difficult aspect about drawing these dogs is to plan carefully the figure's proportions; otherwise, it will look like a cat. Take care with the snout's size when assembling the facial features.

Floppy-eared Dogs

This is the same shape as that drawn on the preceding page. If you fail to capture correctly the external appearance of the floppy ears vis-a-vis the direction that they lie and the extent to which they droop, then the ears will look awkward. Be sure you are thoroughly familiar with how to draw a form layout.

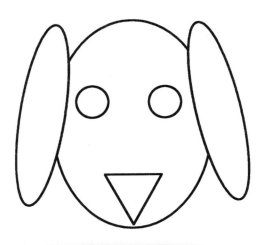

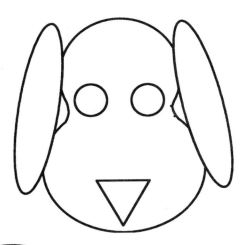

Beagle-Type Dogs

Snoopy helped make all of us familiar with this breed. A main distinguishing feature of beagles is their long, floppy ears. As an excellent means of study practice, I highly recommend that the reader draw such form layouts, keeping these distinguishing features in mind.

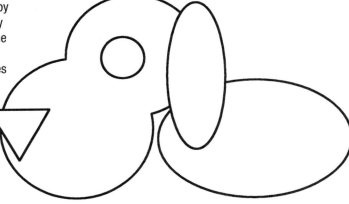

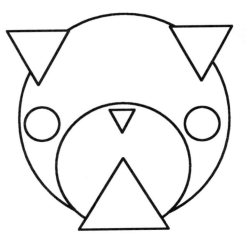

Pugs and Bulldogs

These breeds have wrinkly skin, so they should be depicted outwardly as if having layers and layers of flesh.

A variety of breeds mean that you have to use a variety of shapes!

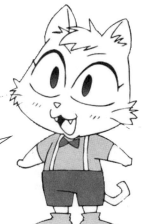

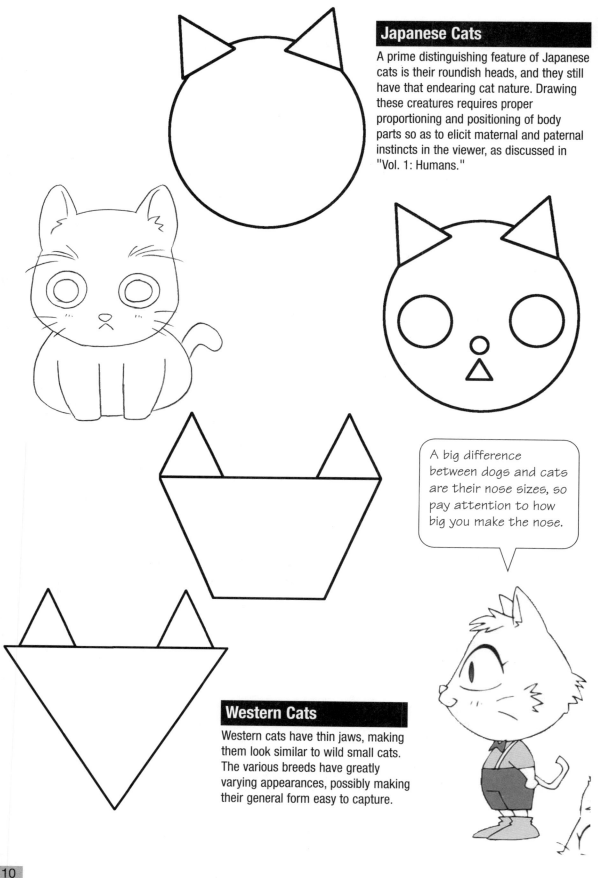

Japanese Cats

A prime distinguishing feature of Japanese cats is their roundish heads, and they still have that endearing cat nature. Drawing these creatures requires proper proportioning and positioning of body parts so as to elicit maternal and paternal instincts in the viewer, as discussed in "Vol. 1: Humans."

A big difference between dogs and cats are their nose sizes, so pay attention to how big you make the nose.

Western Cats

Western cats have thin jaws, making them look similar to wild small cats. The various breeds have greatly varying appearances, possibly making their general form easy to capture.

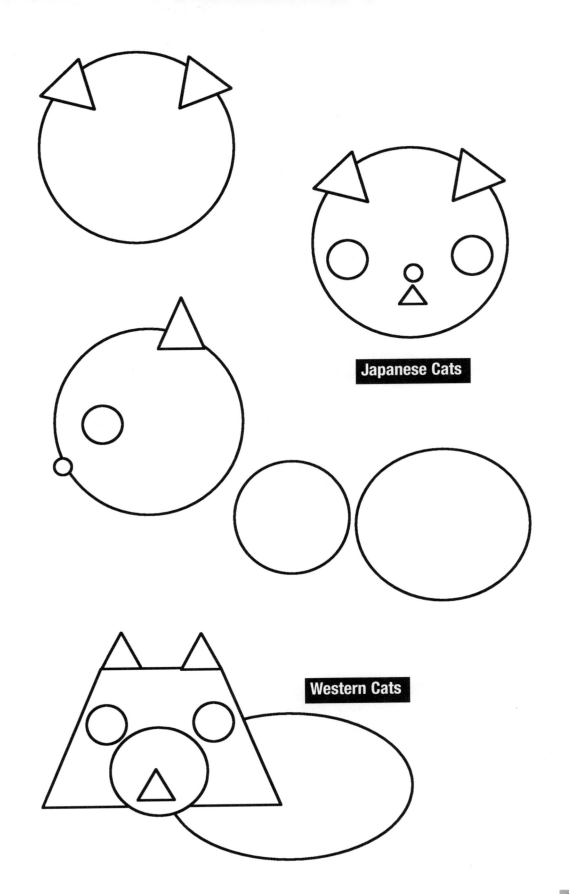

Japanese Cats

Western Cats

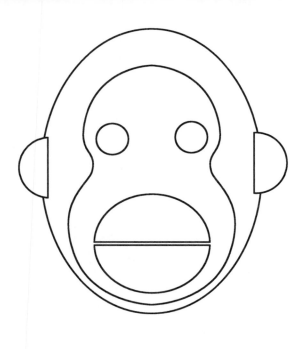

Monkeys

Since monkeys resemble us, they may be proportioned similar to the human figure. Points of consideration are the hairline/fur line and the protruding upper and lower jaw.

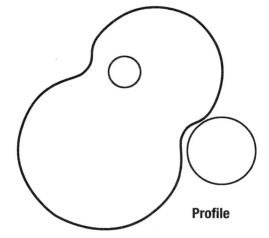

Profile

Orangutans

When you look at a photo, what attracts your attention? You focus on the expanse of the forehead, of course. Modifying the forehead's proportioning from that of the monkey allows you to produce a more convincing "orangutan" look.

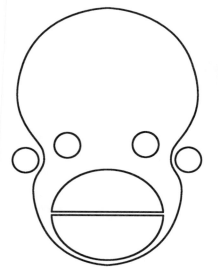

Gorillas

Let's again consider how this animal differs from the monkey visually. The gorilla is built thicker from jaw to neck, and the forehead has a rugged, beefy appearance. These elements should be considered when devising the form layout.

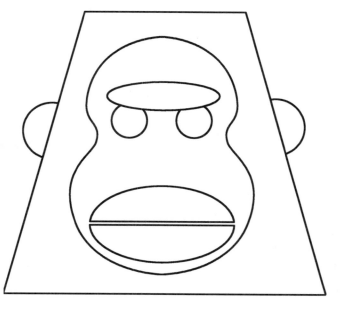

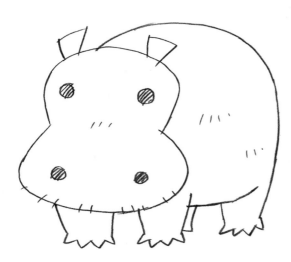

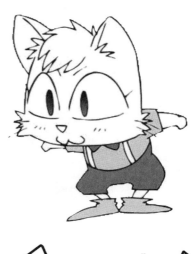

Hippos

Hippopotamuses have large, gourd-shaped heads. The facial features should all lack angles, and the nostrils should be large.

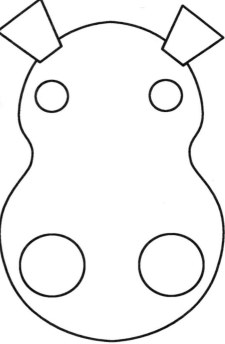

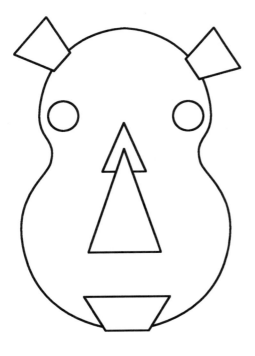

Rhinos

Because the rhinoceros has horns—a major distinguishing trait—this creature is easy to depict. While some people do occasionally hold misconceptions about how many horns the rhino sports, the adult should have two horns to look convincing.

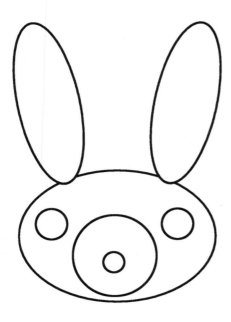

Rabbits

Everyone is familiar with the rabbit's trademark long ears. Some rabbits also have lop ears; however, provided that you have positioned the ears properly and captured the physical appearance reasonably well, this should not pose a problem.

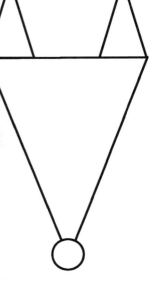

Foxes

Foxes are canines. Thus, they should be designed using the same general appearance as a dog, but care should be taken to give the character the fox's distinctive long face.

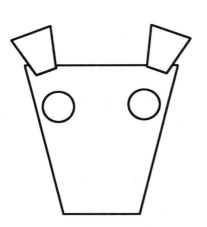

Horses

We tend to associate the phrase "horsey face" with comedians or people with long faces. However, if you look at an actual horse's face, granted it is long, but it is also quite handsome.

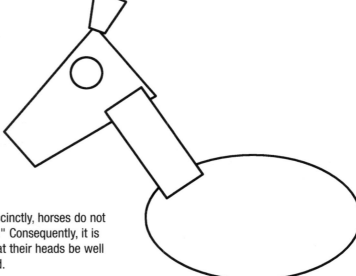

To put it succinctly, horses do not look "dumb." Consequently, it is essential that their heads be well proportioned.

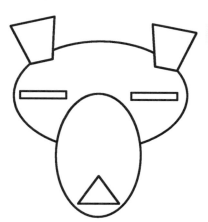

Camels

A camel's face has generally the same appearance as a giraffe but with differently shaped ears. Consequently, the artist must accurately capture the camel's ears, or the camel will come out looking like a giraffe.

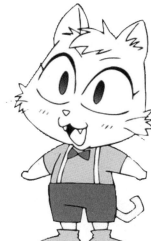

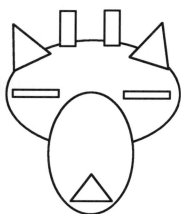

Giraffes

The giraffe has horns and ears that are shaped differently from those of a camel. Failure to capture these features accurately could result in your giraffe looking embarrassingly like a camel (grin).

Bears

We tend to think of bears as scary animals, but in actuality, they have round faces and an endearing look about them. As a result, I recommend giving your bears cute, round faces, provided that there is no particular reason you need to make them look scary.

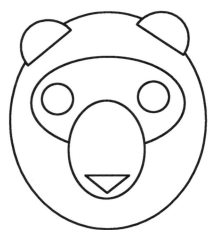

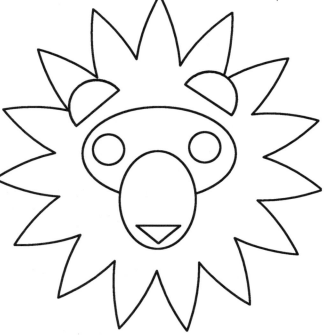

Lions

As you can tell from the figure, the interior facial features closely resemble those of the bear, which leads us to conclude that really the most important feature of the lion is his mane.

Birds

From the perspective of enabling flight and reducing air resistance, I recommend that you conceive of birds as formed fundamentally of rounded shapes.

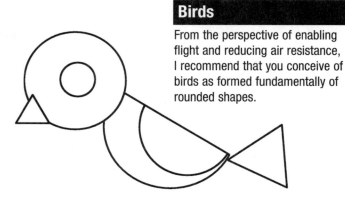

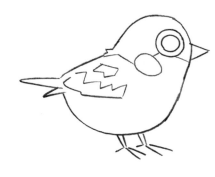

Alligators and Iguanas

When drawing animals with long bodies, including snakes, consideration must be given to the entire external appearance, which should be divided into a head, a trunk, and a tail.

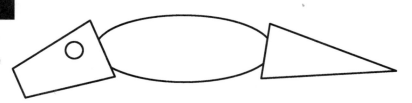

Whales

Illustrations of whales can often be found about town depicted using semicircles. Personally, I feel this is perfectly adequate.

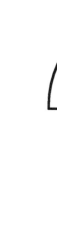

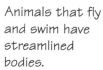

Animals that fly and swim have streamlined bodies.

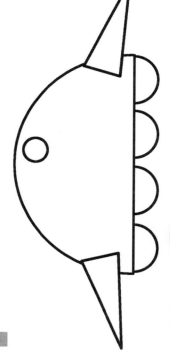

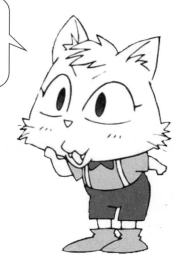

Mola Molas (Ocean Sun Fish)

The Mola mola, which we can find in aquariums, has an immediately recognizable shape. Other than the fins, simply drawing a semicircle creates a suitably shaped Mola mola.

What is anthropomorphism?

Anthropomorphism generally falls into two categories: the dressing of animals in clothes and having them engage in "human" acts, but with the subject primarily retaining its "animal" traits versus an animal behaving in such a "human" manner that it virtually seems like a human pretending to be an animal. Abundant anthropomorphized animals appear in foreign movies, and likely the audience feels a close kinship with animals in a good sense. Sadly, in Japan, despite being a developed nation, awareness of animals' rights is a bit paltry, and many still harbor old-fashioned views regarding service dogs (Seeing Eye dogs, etc.). Even if an animal was anthropomorphized for the very purpose of making it more seem more accessible, that does not necessarily mean the audience will feel closer to the species. Other examples of superb works including anthropomorphism can be found in "Junguru taitei" (Kimba the White Lion) and "Hustle Punch," as well as in various Studio Ghibli titles.

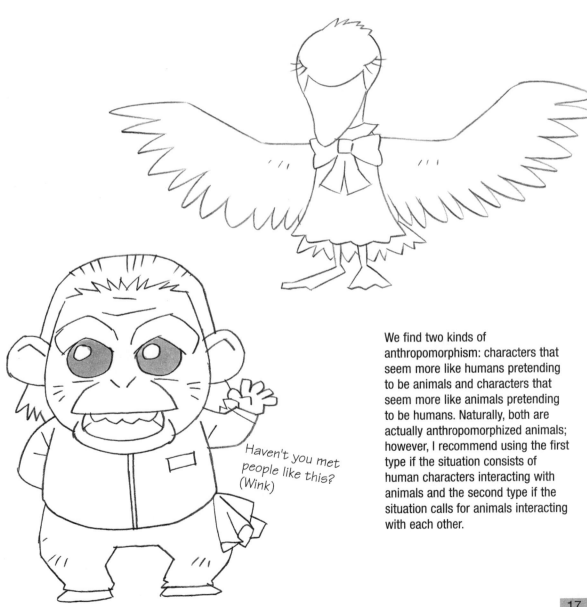

Haven't you met people like this? (Wink)

We find two kinds of anthropomorphism: characters that seem more like humans pretending to be animals and characters that seem more like animals pretending to be humans. Naturally, both are actually anthropomorphized animals; however, I recommend using the first type if the situation consists of human characters interacting with animals and the second type if the situation calls for animals interacting with each other.

For a while in Japan, girls with kitty cat ears were all the rage, and everyone debated whether these characters were cats that had become girls or girls that had taken on a catlike traits. At either rate, it is probably safe to regard this as one form of anthropomorphism. However, the truth of the matter is that since this style of character became popular, it seemed like in the majority of cases, artists were sticking kitty ears on anyone and anything. This does not mean that a girl with kitty cat ears was necessarily a poorly designed character. Rather, what I would like you to consider is that attaching cat ears allows the artist to portray aspects that would normally be difficult with a regular human or imbue the character with individualistic, eccentric qualities. However, because at least two decades have passed since a girl with kitty cat ears first made her appearance, can we really consider such a character "individualistic"?

I probably would never use an animal as a fabric design motif. Suppose that a manga with frog print clothing became popular? If that were the case, I would not want to make all of the characters in a manga of mine dressed in frog motif clothing, as that would detract from their individuality, and, in a worst-case scenario, could constitute a copyright infringement. I would hope that the reader would not become the sort of artist who would design copycat characters that mimic already existing characters by other professional artists.

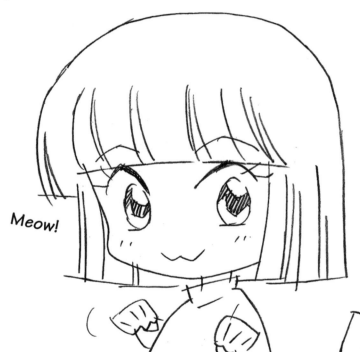

Meow!

There is nothing particularly wrong with a cat-eared girl. As mentioned in "Vol. 1: Humans," the addition of cat ears does not do anything to define the character's personality. Therefore, provided that the character you stick the cat ears on is not the main character, if you are attempting to make a sidekick or peripheral character more appealing, or adding the ears to a character for a single panel as a one-punch visual gag, or when designing a manga featuring animals, then cats ears seem an acceptable touch. Granted, my words will fall on deaf ears for those that find this sort of thing appealing, but the majority of people out there feel surfeited by such characters.

Chapter 2

Turning Animals into Super-Deformed Characters

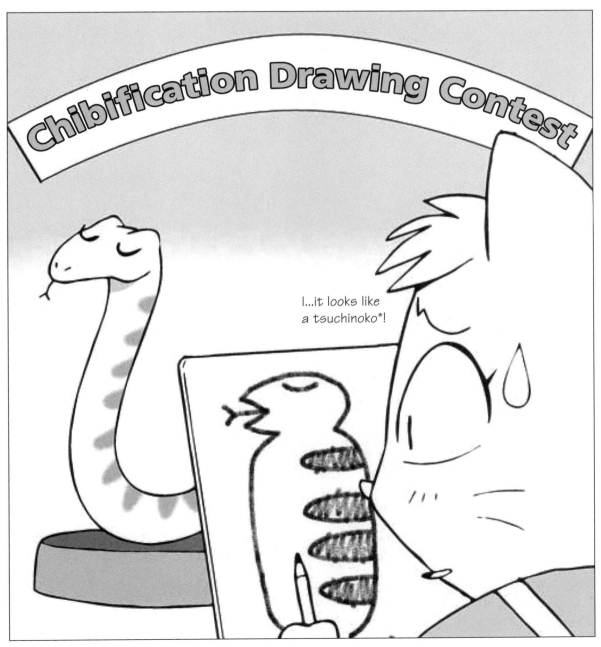

*Tsuchinoko is a highly elusive or possibly mythological creature
with no legs, like a snake, and a head shaped like a mallet.

Dogs

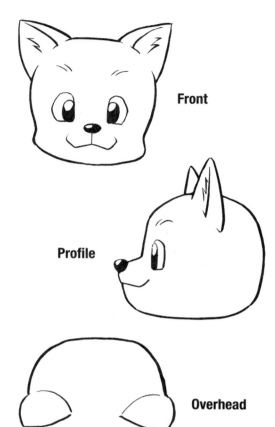

Front

Chibi Character

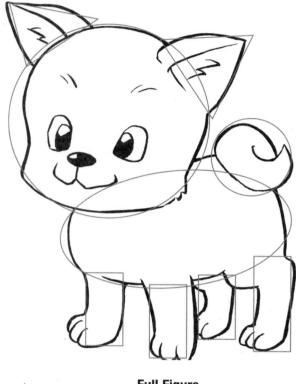

Full Figure

Profile

Overhead

Degrees of Stylization

Degrees of stylization were also covered in Volume 1. Super-deformed (i.e. ultra-stylized) characters are not discrete units, but rather one component to an inner, cohesive manga world. When designing a chibi, the character must match the degree of stylization of the background setting and other characters inhabiting this world. Consequently, a particular ranking of stylization is required for the animals just as it is for the human characters. The artist must stylize the character by simplifying and exaggerating its appearance as deemed necessary to make the character fit its milieu.

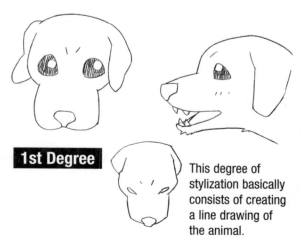

1st Degree

This degree of stylization basically consists of creating a line drawing of the animal.

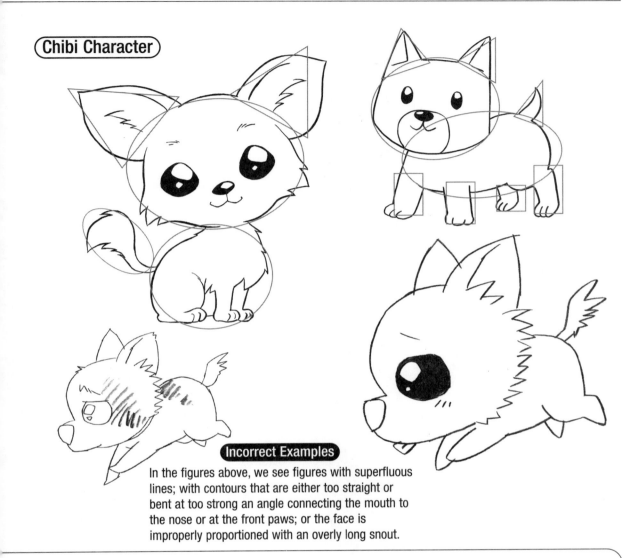

Chibi Character

Incorrect Examples

In the figures above, we see figures with superfluous lines; with contours that are either too straight or bent at too strong an angle connecting the mouth to the nose or at the front paws; or the face is improperly proportioned with an overly long snout.

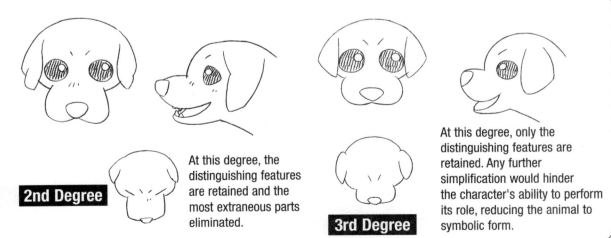

2nd Degree

At this degree, the distinguishing features are retained and the most extraneous parts eliminated.

3rd Degree

At this degree, only the distinguishing features are retained. Any further simplification would hinder the character's ability to perform its role, reducing the animal to symbolic form.

Dogs

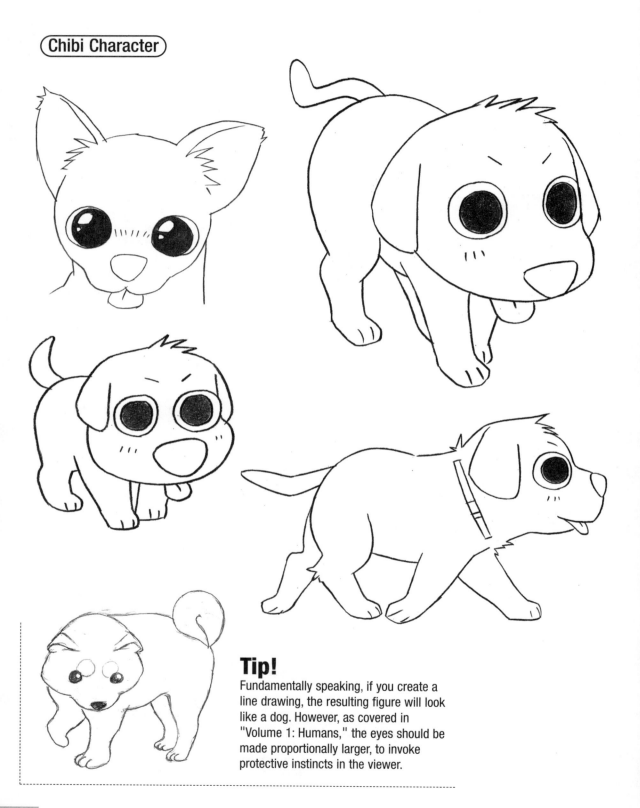

Chibi Character

Tip!

Fundamentally speaking, if you create a
line drawing, the resulting figure will look
like a dog. However, as covered in
"Volume 1: Humans," the eyes should be
made proportionally larger, to invoke
protective instincts in the viewer.

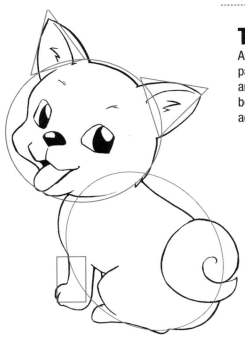

Tip!
As discussed on the previous page, cats, dogs, and other animals that live close to us can be made to look even more adorable by enlarging their eyes.

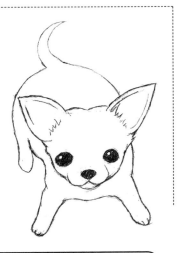

Anthropomorphized Characters
The dogs transformed into people:

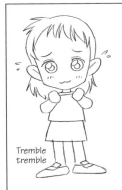

Tremble tremble

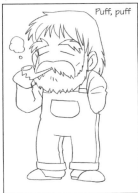

Puff, puff

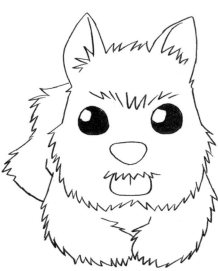

Incorrect Examples
First of all, the fur tufts on this dog are at overly even intervals. In addition, the eyes are proportionally small with respect to the body, making this a poorly balanced chibi, and the eyes are too close together. All in all, this chibi is not going to touch the reader on an instinctive level.

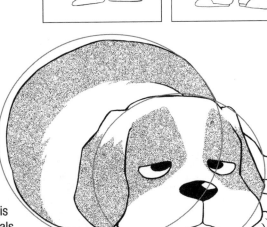

Chibi Character

Cats (All Styles)

Chibi Character

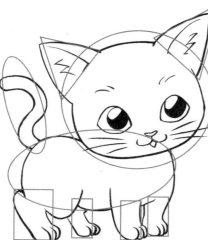

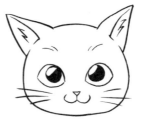

Front

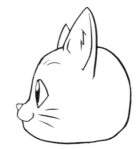

Profile

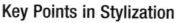

Full Figure

Key Points in Stylization

As with the dog, key points on the cat are the figure's exterior contours and the proportioning of the eyes. I recommend completing the head first and then planning the full figure's proportions.

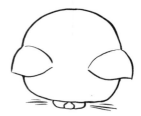

Overhead

Anthropomorphized Character

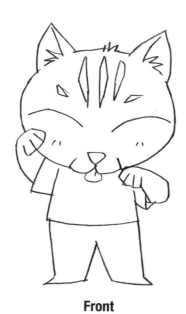

Front

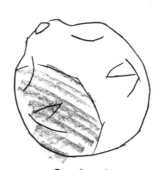

Side

Overhead

Key Points in Anthropomorphization

When anthropomorphizing a character, first establish whether the character will be primarily human or primarily animal. Decide whether the character will be a person-like cat or a catlike person, and then design your character.

Japanese Cats (Shorthair)

Chibi Character

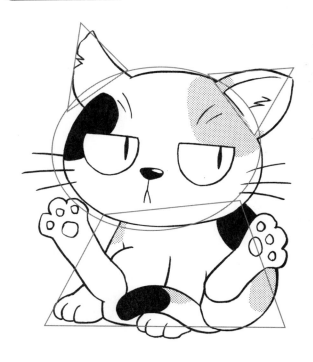

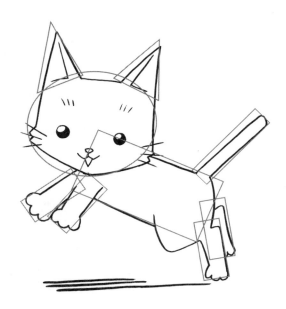

Anthropomorphized Character

Cats are flexible.
Purrrr.

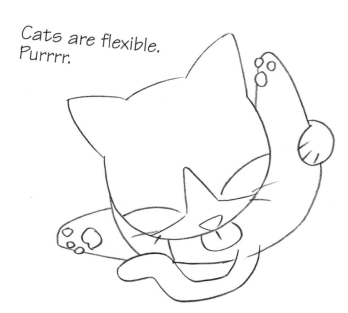

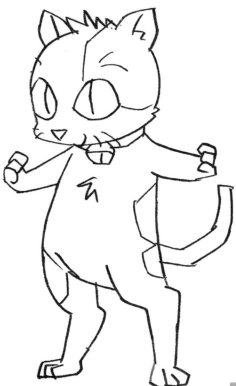

25

Western Cats (Shorthair)

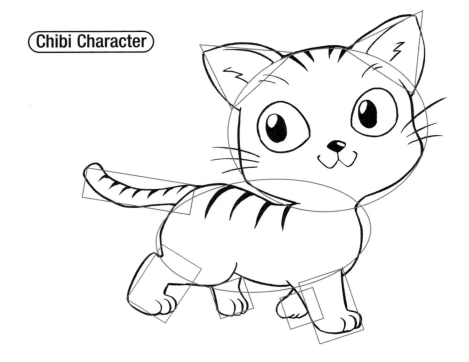

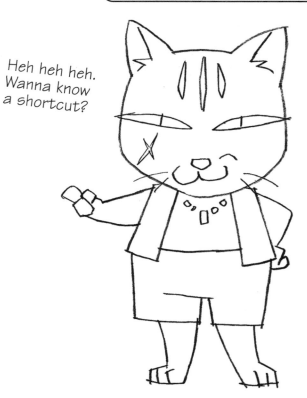

Heh heh heh. Wanna know a shortcut?

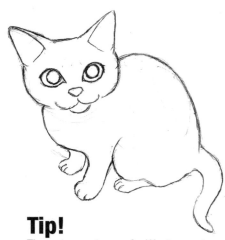

Tip!
The outer contours of a Western cat distinguish the cat on many levels. Therefore, careful attention must be paid to the contours when devising the body's proportions so that they will match the head.

Western Cats (Longhair)

Chibi Character

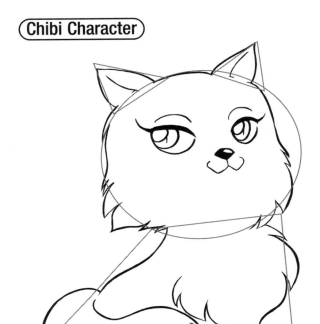

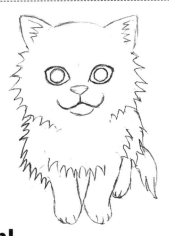

Tip!

Naturally, the fur's length is the most characteristic feature of a longhaired cat, making how to render the cat's coat a critical issue. What generally results in the best-looking character is to minimize the volume and to suggest the fur's quality or texture.

Anthropomorphized Character

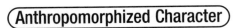

Money is everything, dahling.

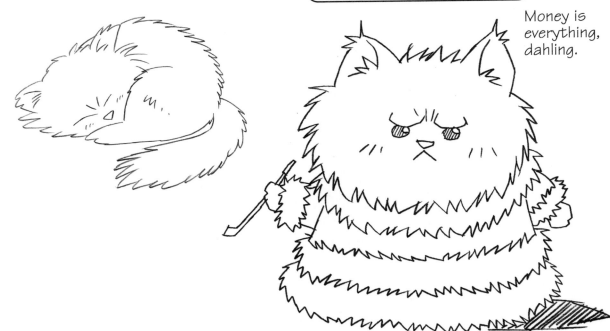

What part of the animal should I stylize to create a chibi character?

Answer

Typically, artists exaggerate any physical features that allow us to identify the animal readily (e.g. the long trunk of a dachshund). The next most common features to exaggerate are personality traits or idiosyncratic qualities the animal possesses (e.g. look about the eyes, facial expression, physical habits, for example if an animal has a strong sense of justice, then it is drawn holding itself erect, or conversely, if it is a villainous character, then it is shown leaning, etc.). The addition of such portrayals brings the character to life.

Dogs

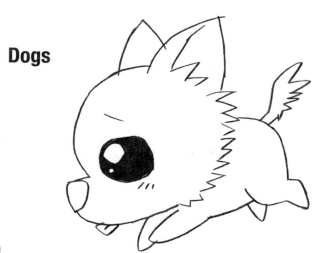

Key Point!
Sometimes merely enlarging the head and eyes to a certain extent is enough to make the animal look cute. If you overuse the technique, you do risk your reader feeling oversaturated and losing interest.

Key Point!
This point applies to both cats and dogs: short legs produce a cuter, more "chibi" look than long.

Cats

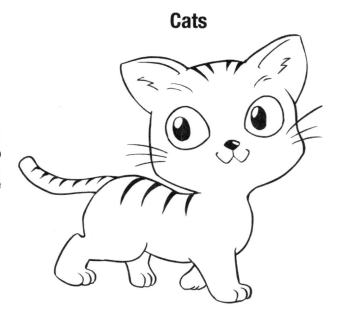

If you follow these guides, you should be able to produce chibi characters to some extent. However, ultimately, you will need to research properly into the skeletal structure and other physical aspects of the animals.

Because overall balance is important, I highly recommend that you practice stylizing figures and achieving the proper proportions.

How should I handle the whiskers? (My animals keep losing their appeal.)

Answer

I can't help but wonder if you are adding too many whiskers or making them too long or too thick. Consider how critical the whiskers are as a distinguishing feature. While this does depend on the degree of stylization, whiskers are indispensable to a cat's survival. Consequently, a chibi cat will look more convincing if it has whiskers rather than not. In contrast, humans find it difficult to grasp exactly what a dog does with its whiskers—mind you, I'm not suggesting that dogs have no need for them. As a result, artists often omit whiskers when drawing dogs (although, this is not always the case). Next, all you need to do is figure what whisker volume and length matches the degree of stylization. This depends on the artist's personal taste, so I recommend drawing several dozens of patterns to experiment and adjust them to see what actually looks best to you.

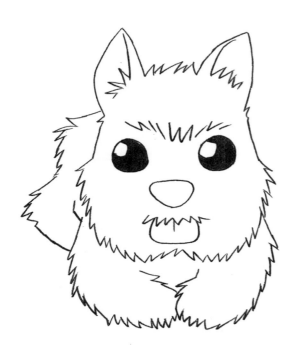

Key Point!

Whiskers tend to look better if you draw them shorter than they would be in reality. (If the animal has long hair, then you may omit them altogether.). I have tried to drive this point home several times now, but in super-deformed characters, "long" is taboo. Naturally, drawing something on the long side occasionally becomes necessary to the presentation; however, on a character's body, all long things should be made short.

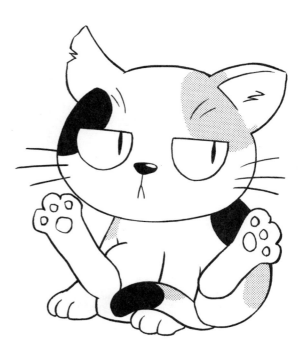

Hamsters

Chibi Character

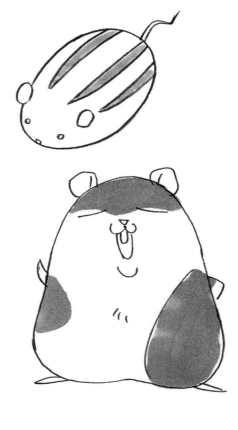

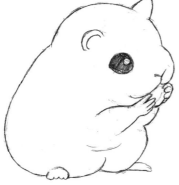

Tip!
Hamsters are such easy characters to create that we see them pop up in a countless manga. The most critical issue here is to distill your line use down to only those necessary. These characters look better if lines suggesting skin folds or muscle contours are omitted.

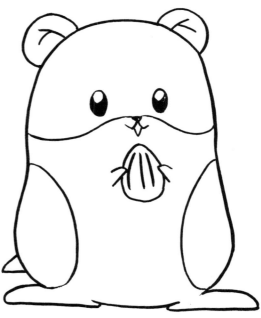

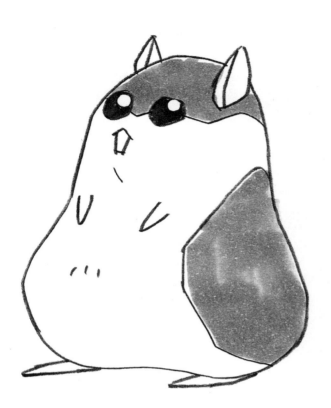

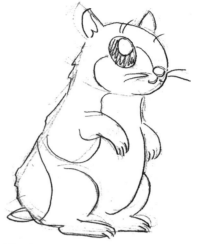

Tip!

Whiskers are commonly longer than the animal's face. However, long whiskers just throw off the balance on a chibi character. It is vital that you draw the whiskers at a length that suits the face's overall proportions.

Anthropomorphized Character

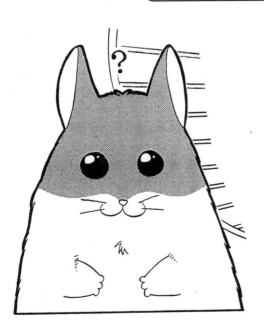

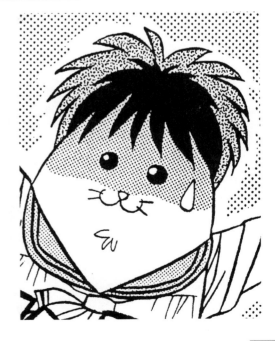

Rabbits

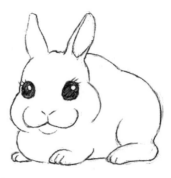

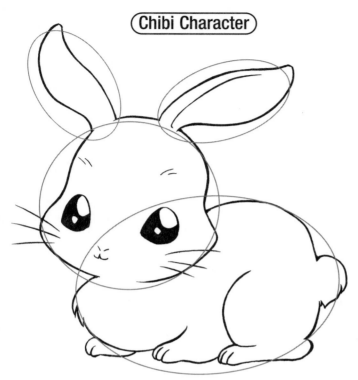

Chibi Character

Tip!
While long ears are a rabbit's distinguishing features, in reality rabbits' ears are not as long as they appear in manga. This does not necessarily mean that retaining the ears' natural length will lend itself to a chibi character. In fact, the opposite is the case. It is vital that you consider the figure's overall proportions and adjust the ears' length as needed.

Anthropomorphized Character

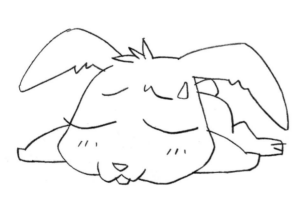

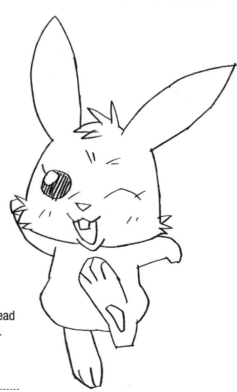

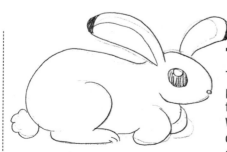

Tip!
This is an extremely basic point. To the left, we see a head that is too small for the body. When drawing, be sure you double check the figure's overall balance.

Squirrels and Chipmunks

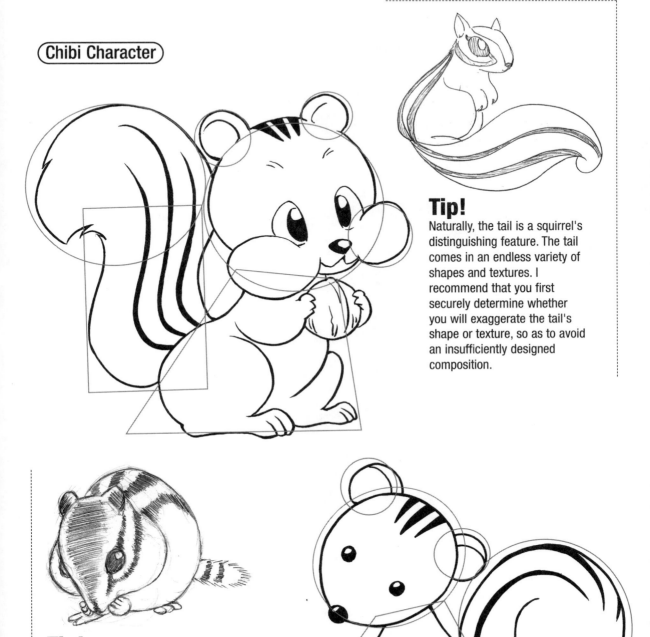

Tip!

Naturally, the tail is a squirrel's distinguishing feature. The tail comes in an endless variety of shapes and textures. I recommend that you first securely determine whether you will exaggerate the tail's shape or texture, so as to avoid an insufficiently designed composition.

Tip!

Small animals tend to have a stylized look about them from the get-go, and sometimes simplifying them seems like an onerous task. How to handle the stylization of these creatures constitutes a key issue. Once again, I ask you to take careful note of how the distinguishing features have been captured.

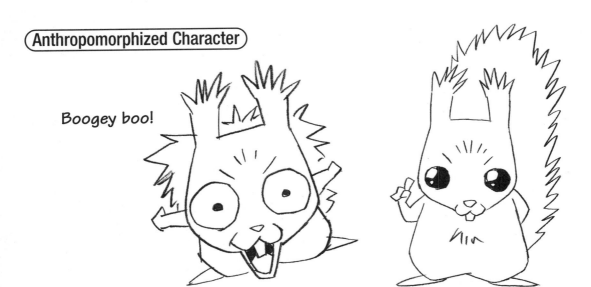

Anthropomorphized Character

Boogey boo!

Ferrets

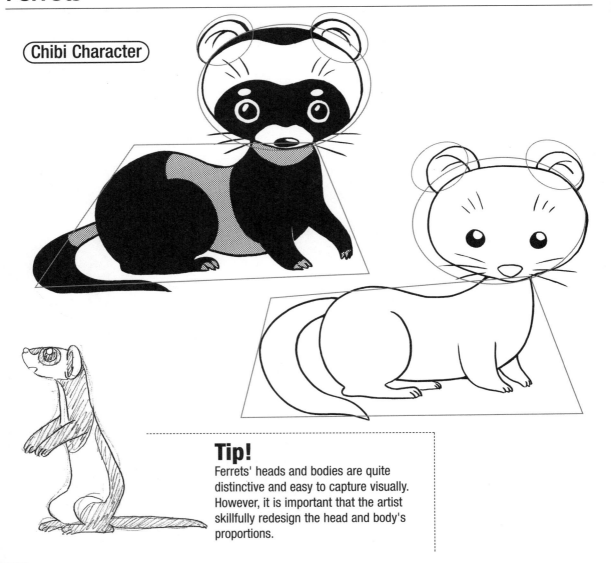

Chibi Character

Tip!
Ferrets' heads and bodies are quite distinctive and easy to capture visually. However, it is important that the artist skillfully redesign the head and body's proportions.

Prairie Dogs

Chibi Character

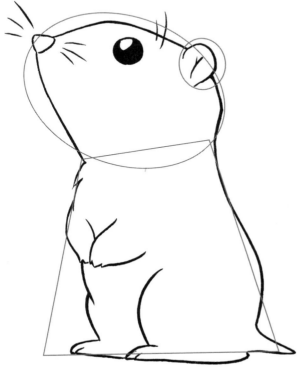

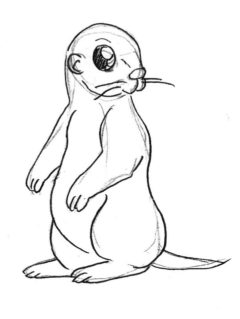

Don't worry about me.
I'm fine.

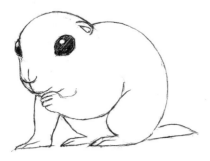

Tip!

If you take a good, long look at a prairie dog, you will
find characteristics of various other animals. They bear
a resemblance to hamsters, guinea pigs, squirrels, and
other rodents. If you find yourself banging your head
against a wall trying to capture an animal's
distinguishing features, sometimes amplifying various
subtle characteristics works. Design the character
according to the situation or scene.

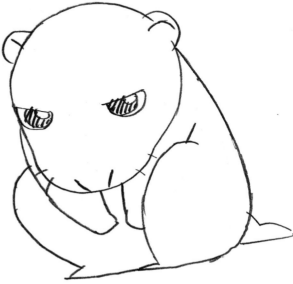

Anthropomorphized Character

Mice

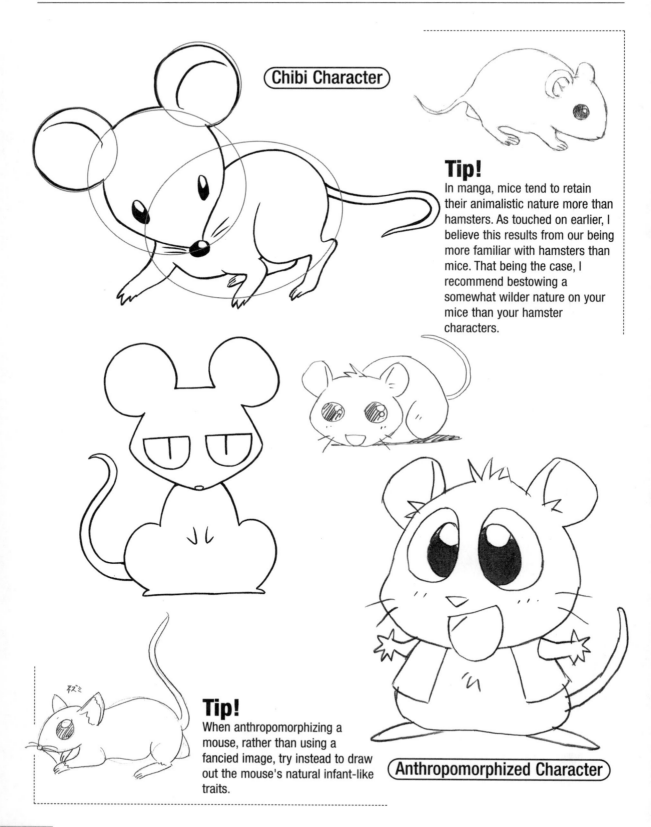

Chibi Character

Tip!

In manga, mice tend to retain their animalistic nature more than hamsters. As touched on earlier, I believe this results from our being more familiar with hamsters than mice. That being the case, I recommend bestowing a somewhat wilder nature on your mice than your hamster characters.

Tip!

When anthropomorphizing a mouse, rather than using a fancied image, try instead to draw out the mouse's natural infant-like traits.

Anthropomorphized Character

Monkeys

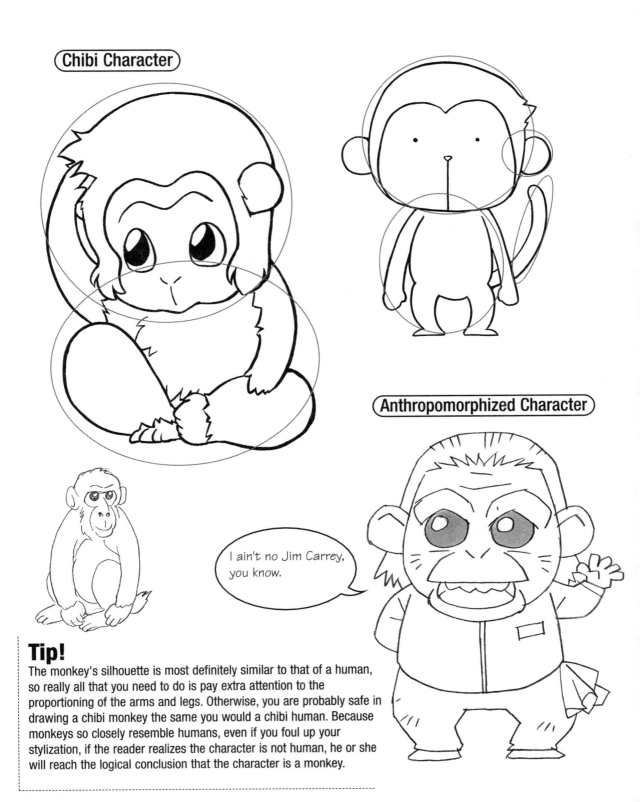

Chibi Character

Anthropomorphized Character

I ain't no Jim Carrey, you know.

Tip!
The monkey's silhouette is most definitely similar to that of a human, so really all that you need to do is pay extra attention to the proportioning of the arms and legs. Otherwise, you are probably safe in drawing a chibi monkey the same you would a chibi human. Because monkeys so closely resemble humans, even if you foul up your stylization, if the reader realizes the character is not human, he or she will reach the logical conclusion that the character is a monkey.

Foxes

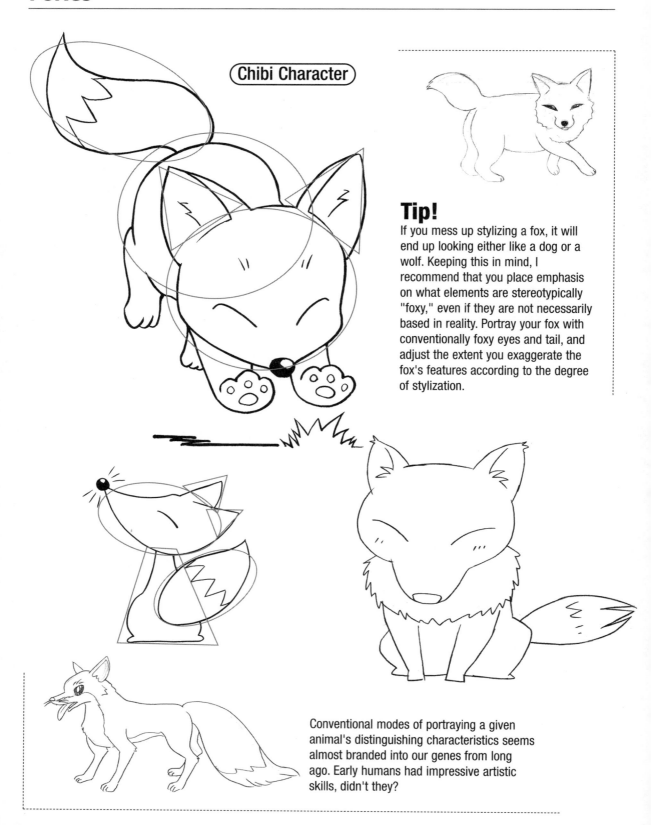

Chibi Character

Tip!

If you mess up stylizing a fox, it will end up looking either like a dog or a wolf. Keeping this in mind, I recommend that you place emphasis on what elements are stereotypically "foxy," even if they are not necessarily based in reality. Portray your fox with conventionally foxy eyes and tail, and adjust the extent you exaggerate the fox's features according to the degree of stylization.

Conventional modes of portraying a given animal's distinguishing characteristics seems almost branded into our genes from long ago. Early humans had impressive artistic skills, didn't they?

Raccoon Dogs

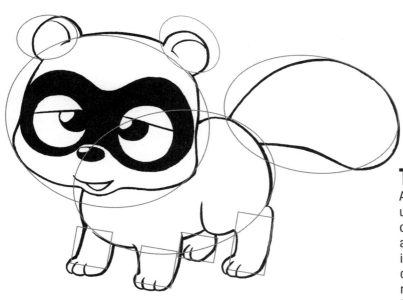

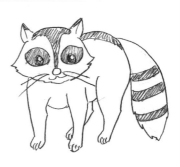

Tip!

As we did on the previous page, let us consider for a moment what characteristics distinguish this animal. When you see a raccoon dog in a zoo, does it have a bulging, drum-like belly? Were the male raccoon dogs as well endowed as the raccoon dog knickknacks people use to decorate their homes? The answer is no on all counts, right? And yet, when we hear the name "raccoon dog," these tend to be the characteristics that first pop into our heads. If you were to draw a raccoon dog as it really looked, the resulting character would appear undernourished and a cross between a raccoon and a lesser panda. To prevent the reader's confusion, it is vital that you draw on the traditional, stereotypical characteristics handed down to us by our ancestors.

Anthropomorphized Character

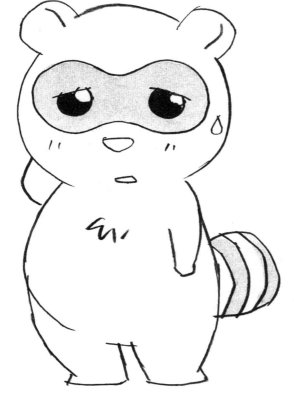

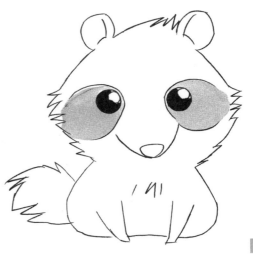

Seals and Hedgehogs

Chibi Character

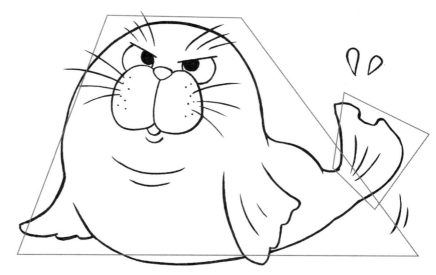

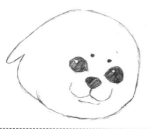

Tip!

Suppose you successfully create a stylized rendition of the seal's characteristically large head, but then foul up simplification of the seal's body. Now your efforts are for naught. Visualize the overall form before you begin to draw.

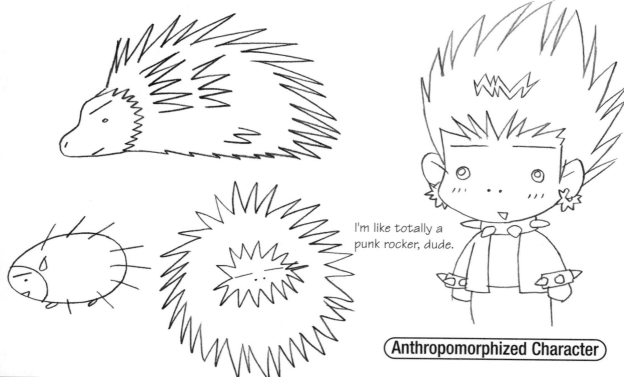

I'm like totally a punk rocker, dude.

Anthropomorphized Character

How should I make my chibi characters walk and run?

Answer

If in the degree of stylization used the animal has clearly retained its joints, then you merely need to show the animal running, as it would normally using those joints. If owing to the degree of stylization, the animal has lost its joints, then draw upon the basic appearance of the animal when running: show the front and legs spread apart or close, show the animal alternating right forward left back and vice versa, or show the legs moving in the same direction at the same time. Investigate how each animal looks when it runs, trying to identify those features that distinguish the species. Moreover, each animal has differently constructed joints, and there are some ranges of motion physically infeasible for some animals, requiring that you familiarize yourself with the various species' skeletal structures.

Walking on Four Legs

Walking on Two Legs

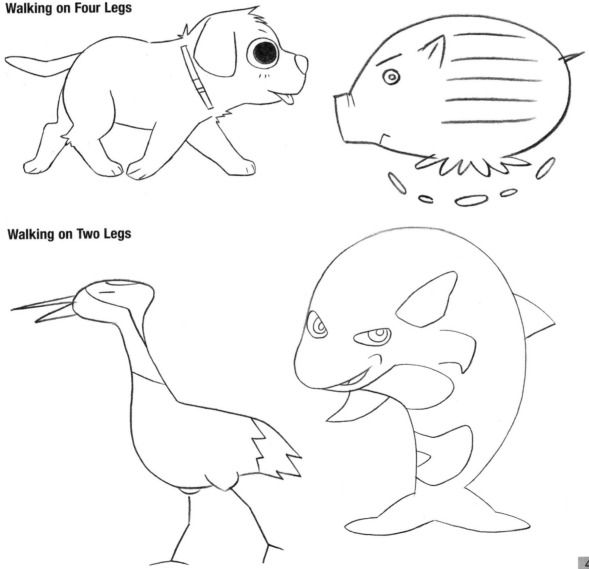

Koalas and Otters

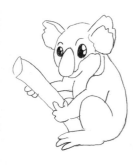

Tip!

Occasionally, drawing a creature with large eyes will make it more endearing. However, in the case of koalas, because they have their characteristically large nose, the large eyes and nose compete with each other, destroying the face's balance. I recommend drawing koalas with small eyes.

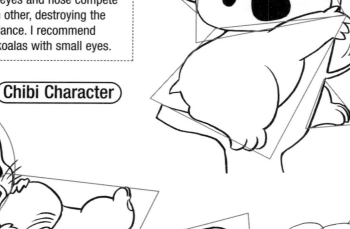

(Chibi Character)

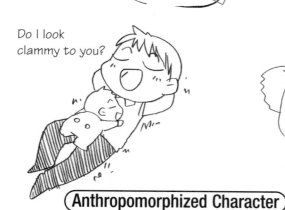

Do I look clammy to you?

(Anthropomorphized Character)

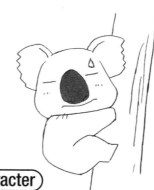

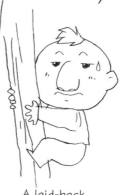

A laid-back koala-guy, or just a plain old sloth?

Tip!

While this is probably just a misconception, we seem to picture otters perpetually holding a shell of some sort. Consequently, exaggerating this trait makes the character more convincing.

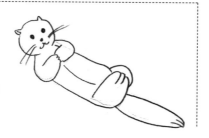

Horses

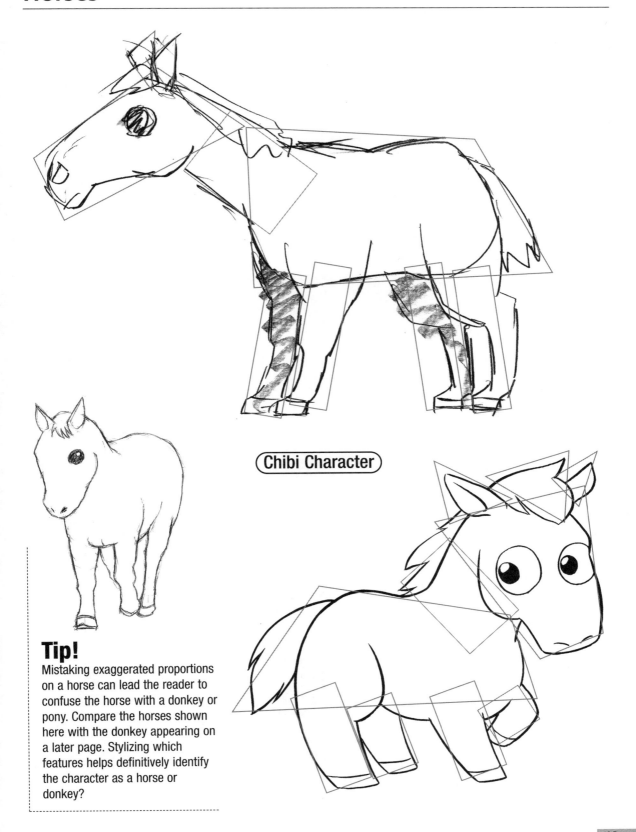

Chibi Character

Tip!
Mistaking exaggerated proportions on a horse can lead the reader to confuse the horse with a donkey or pony. Compare the horses shown here with the donkey appearing on a later page. Stylizing which features helps definitively identify the character as a horse or donkey?

Horses

Anthropomorphized Character

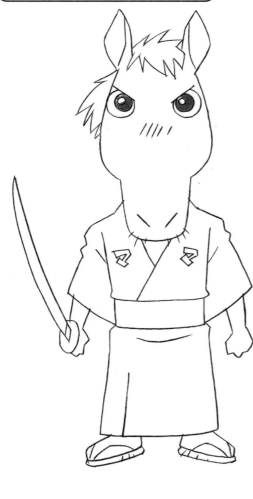

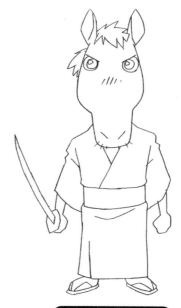

Incorrect Examples

This figure is poorly proportioned. The proportioning from the underarm (which is based on the shoulders' positioning) to the trunk and the angle of these lines has been badly handled. The obi (sash) arcs downward, sapping the figure of its vigor. The legs appear parallel to one another, causing the figure to lose any sense of weight. This is just a miserably balanced composition.

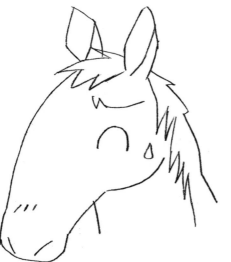

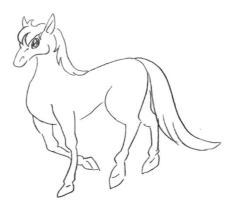

Tip!

You can certainly design a chibi character simply by exaggerating certain features; however, the figure's overall proportional balance is still important. You should always reassess the full figure's balance after you have assembled the individual parts you elected to exaggerate. Achieving proportional balance is a delicate matter. In the anthropomorphized figure above, minor mistakes in proportioning destroyed the figure's overall visual balance.

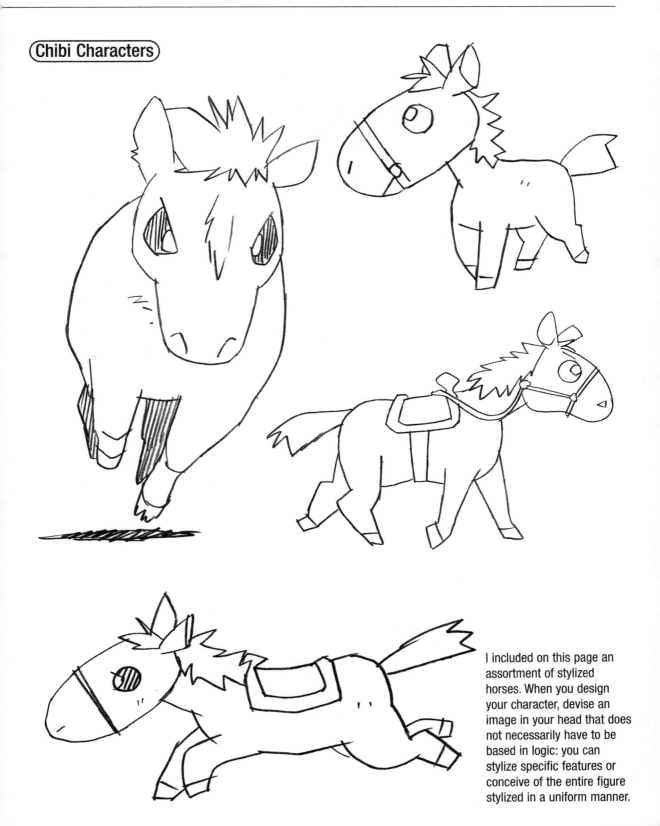

Chibi Characters

I included on this page an assortment of stylized horses. When you design your character, devise an image in your head that does not necessarily have to be based in logic: you can stylize specific features or conceive of the entire figure stylized in a uniform manner.

Cows and Bulls

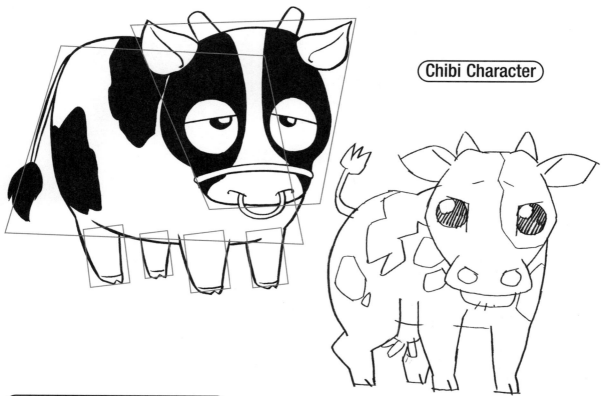

Chibi Character

Anthropomorphized Character

This is what happens, kiddies, when you eat and then go right to sleep afterwards.

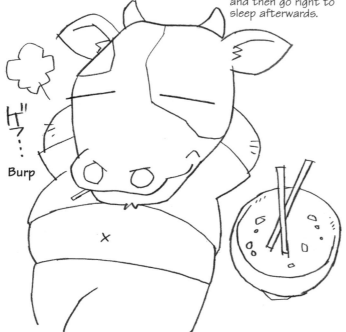

Burp

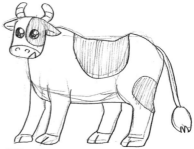

Tip!
The cow has many versatile features, which can be tweaked to create a stylized cow or to look like a human (see top two figures). Please note, however, that if you overemphasize the behemoth aspect of the cow, you could risk your stylized character losing its sense of charm.

Sheep

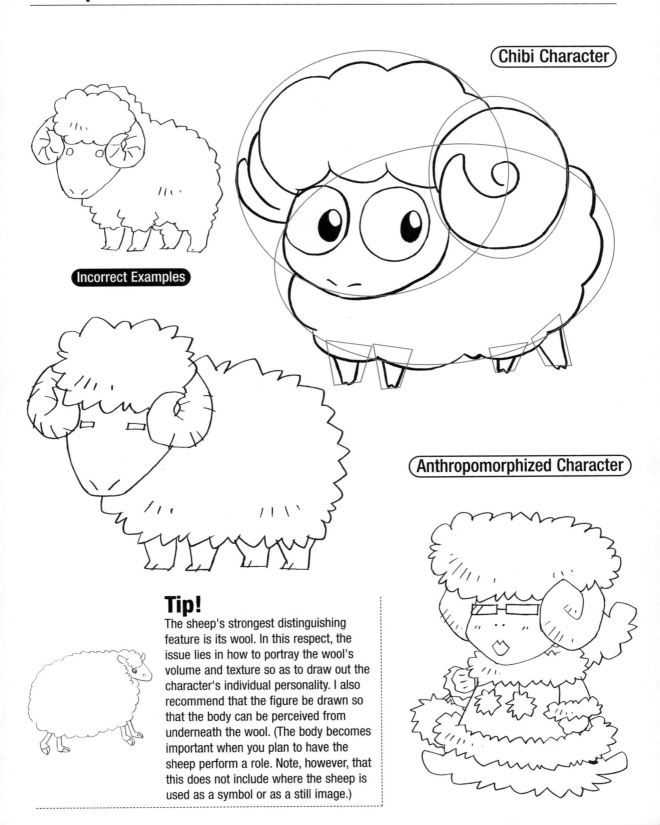

Chibi Character

Incorrect Examples

Anthropomorphized Character

Tip!

The sheep's strongest distinguishing feature is its wool. In this respect, the issue lies in how to portray the wool's volume and texture so as to draw out the character's individual personality. I also recommend that the figure be drawn so that the body can be perceived from underneath the wool. (The body becomes important when you plan to have the sheep perform a role. Note, however, that this does not include where the sheep is used as a symbol or as a still image.)

47

Donkeys

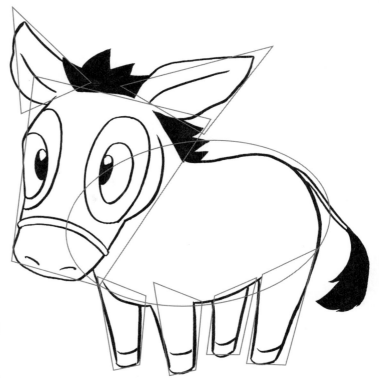

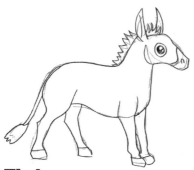

Tip!
Other than the ears and the general build, there are hardly any differences between the horse and the donkey. Be sure to take extra care with exaggerating the ears and body when drawing the donkey.

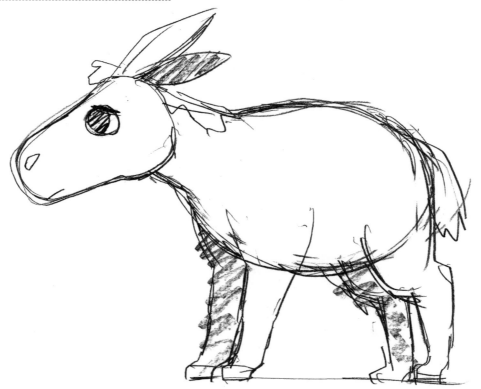

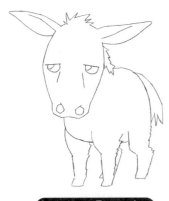

What if you have successfully stylized the ears and the body, but you have not carefully balanced the overall proportions? As a result, the viewer may find it difficult to discern what animal the character is.

The face is derived according to our preconceived notion of what the animal should look like. In the case of a horse, we tend to picture a fast racehorse, while when we think of a donkey, we visualize a peaceful farm animal. Your character should embody these notions.

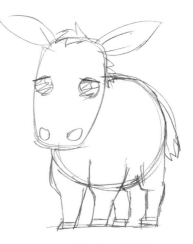

Incorrect Examples

This figure has too much information. Avoid drawing fur tufts in too much detail. The face contains too many lines. It is impossible to make a character look endearing without more simplification. In contrast to the space between the eyes, the distance between the nostrils is just too close to reality. Make an effort to match proportioning to the degree of stylization.

Rough Sketch

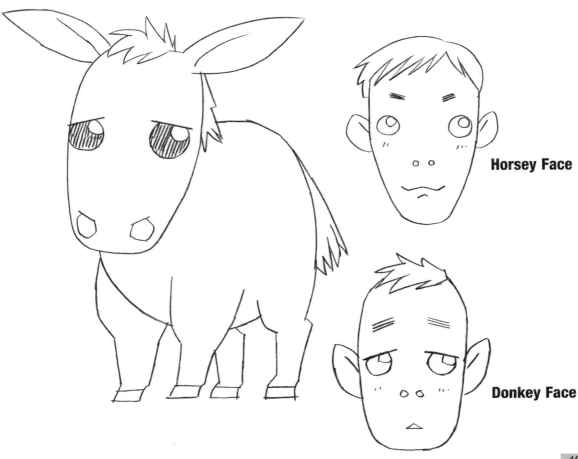

Horsey Face

Donkey Face

Pigs

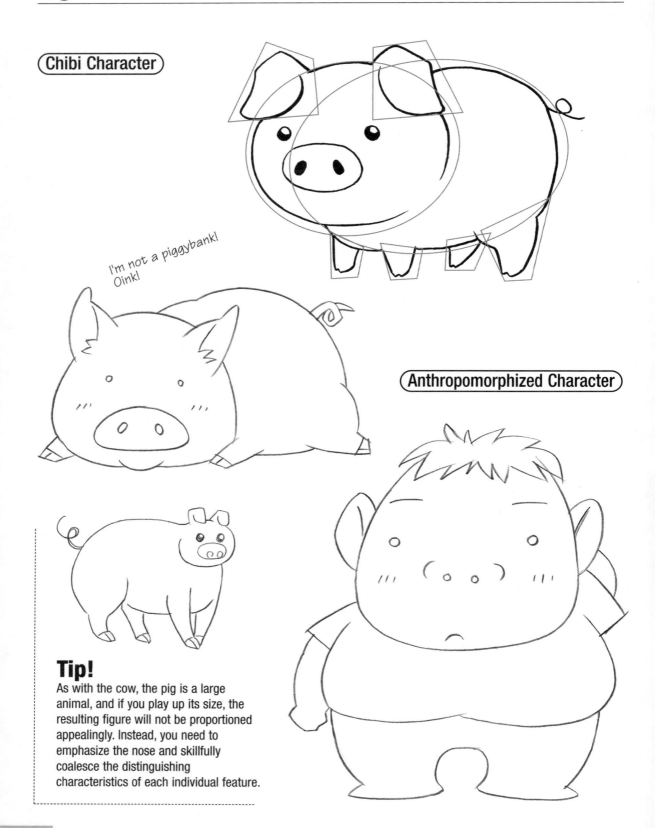

Chibi Character

I'm not a piggybank! Oink!

Anthropomorphized Character

Tip!

As with the cow, the pig is a large animal, and if you play up its size, the resulting figure will not be proportioned appealingly. Instead, you need to emphasize the nose and skillfully coalesce the distinguishing characteristics of each individual feature.

Boars

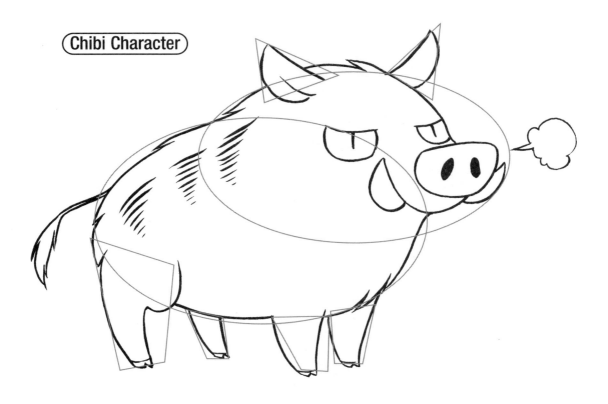

Chibi Character

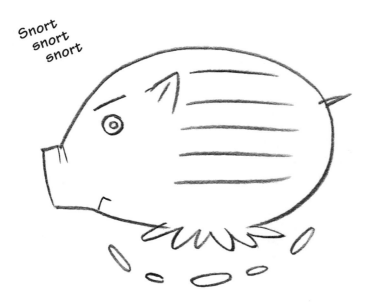

Snort snort snort

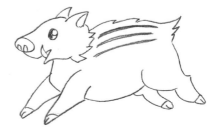

Tip!

A boar is a type of pig. Logically, you should be able to create a satisfying boar by drawing it as a wild pig. Therefore, design the boar with a trimmer, fitter body than the pig. After you have obtained an overall form for your boar, cover it with hair to produce a more convincingly boar-like image.

Goats

Chibi Character

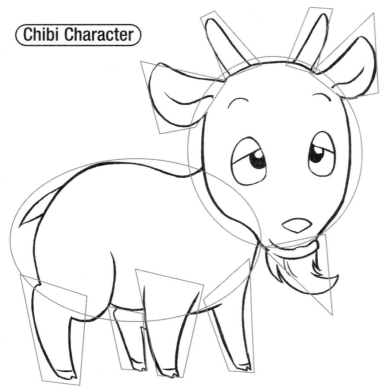

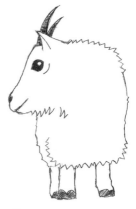

Tip!
The goat has a soft, full beard. Becoming misled by the way the hair is depicted, and the animal's overall proportions can cause the viewer to confuse this creature with a sheep, so be careful.

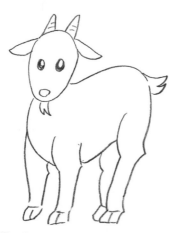

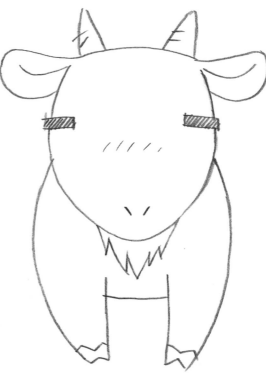

Tip!
You may portray the goat with round eyes. However, one of this animal's distinguishing features is its impish eyes. Shaping the eyes to emphasize this aspect will result in a more convincing goat.

Lions

Chibi Character

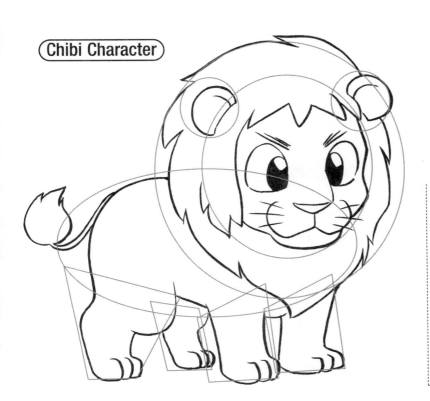

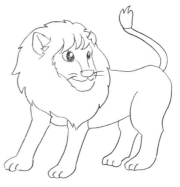

Tip!
The lion's most identifying feature is its mane. Thus, merely adding a mane to a ferocious feline produces a lion. However, by determining whether to draw the mane on a big cat or a cuddly kitten, you may greatly vary the appearance and atmosphere the character projects. Play around with different looks, taking note of each resulting image.

Anthropomorphized Character

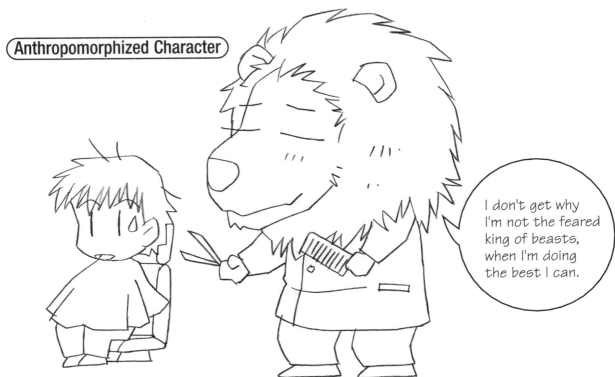

I don't get why I'm not the feared king of beasts, when I'm doing the best I can.

Tigers

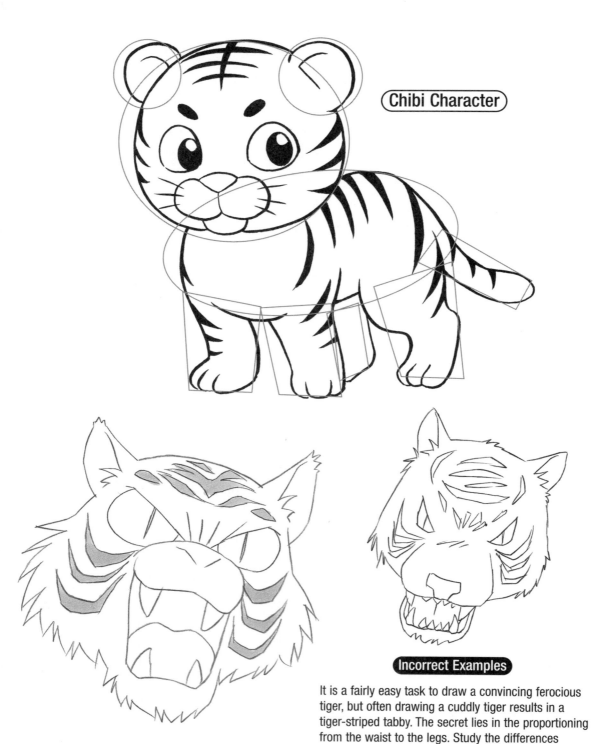

Chibi Character

Incorrect Examples

It is a fairly easy task to draw a convincing ferocious tiger, but often drawing a cuddly tiger results in a tiger-striped tabby. The secret lies in the proportioning from the waist to the legs. Study the differences between the tiger and the housecat and try to capture the difference visually.

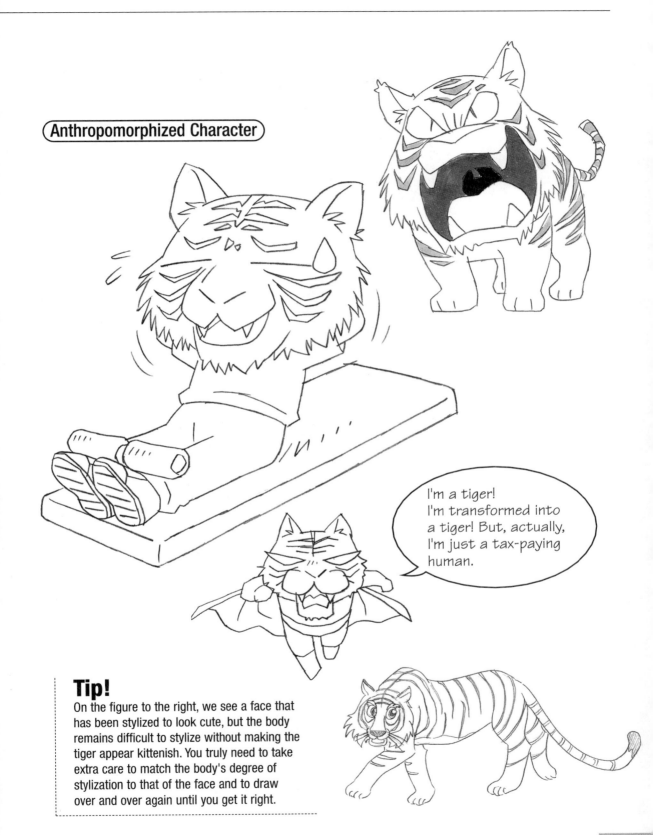

Anthropomorphized Character

I'm a tiger!
I'm transformed into
a tiger! But, actually,
I'm just a tax-paying
human.

Tip!

On the figure to the right, we see a face that
has been stylized to look cute, but the body
remains difficult to stylize without making the
tiger appear kittenish. You truly need to take
extra care to match the body's degree of
stylization to that of the face and to draw
over and over again until you get it right.

Elephants

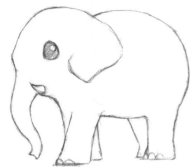

(Chibi Character)

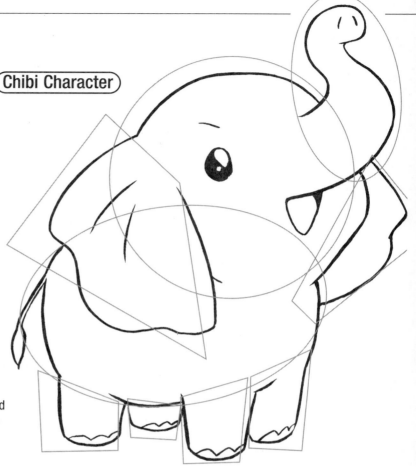

Tip!

The elephant has yet other major distinguishing features, and as discussed earlier, emphasis of the animal's largeness will destroy the overall proportioning of your chibi character. After you have first stylized the elephant's various features, then concentrate your energies on achieving a satisfying visual balance suitable to the degree of stylization used.

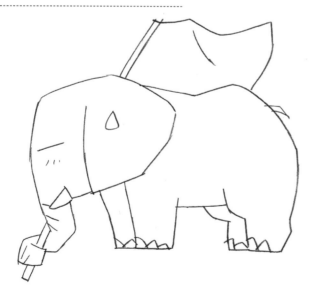

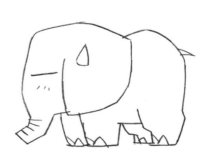

If my nose gets any bigger, I'm in twobble.

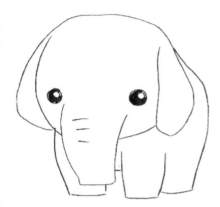

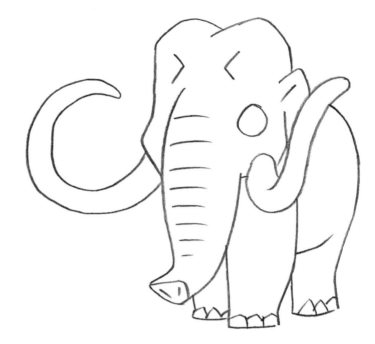

Anthropomorphized Character

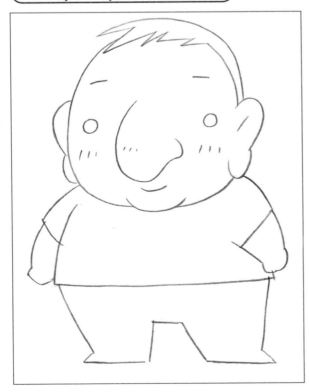

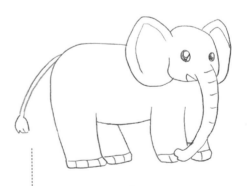

Tip!
When drawing the elephant, do not forget it is a vertebrate and that there is a spine traveling from the neck down its back.

Rhinoceroses

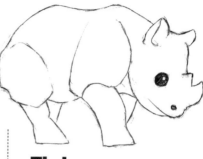

(Chibi Character)

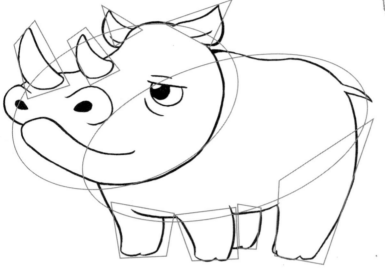

Tip!

If you try to stylize and include too much, the overall composition will look fussy. Be sure you carefully assess which characteristics distinguish the animal and include those.

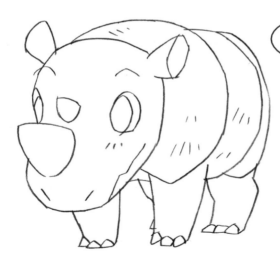

Rhinos are fraidy cats!

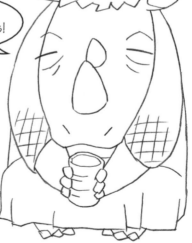

(Anthropomorphized Character)

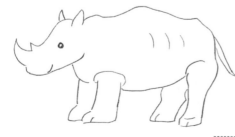

Tip!

In the figure to the left, we see a cute face paired with a realistic body. The artist should always remember to design characters using a uniform degree of stylization.

Hippopotamuses

Chibi Character

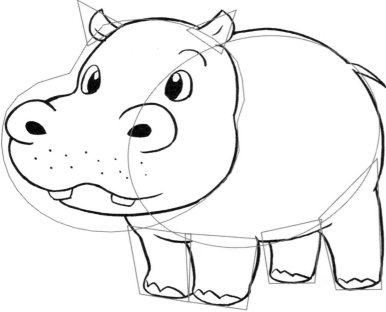

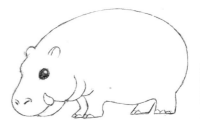

Tip!

This character comes across somehow as if its stylization is not complete. The artist should have been a little more audacious and used more dramatic stylization. Also, note how the stylization of the legs does not match those of the head and body, which the legs seem too thin to support.

A bunch of symbols?

Aaaoum!

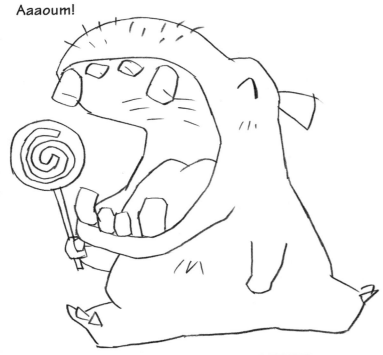

Anthropomorphized Character

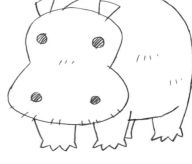

Tip!

Contrary to the figure above it, this figure seems lacking in cuddly characteristics. Try to be more daring in your use of stylization.

Camels

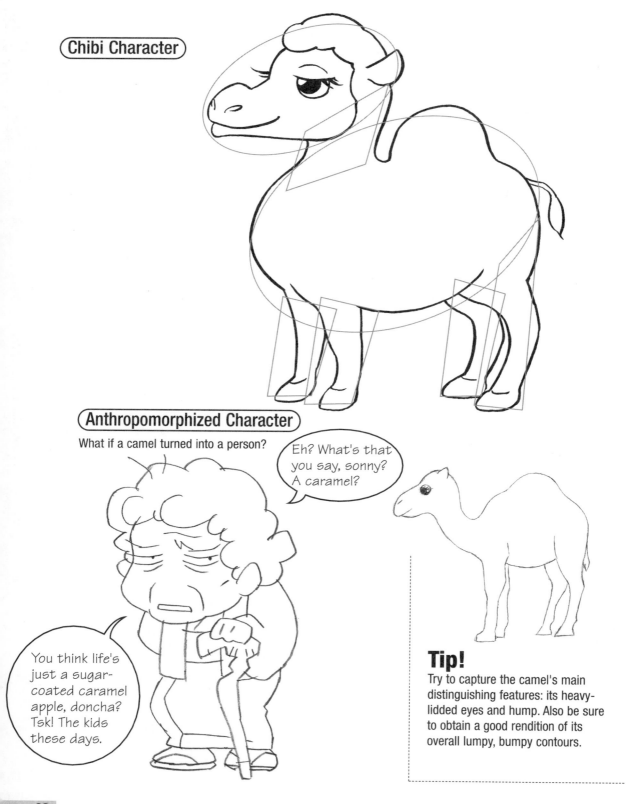

Chibi Character

Anthropomorphized Character

What if a camel turned into a person?

Eh? What's that you say, sonny? A caramel?

You think life's just a sugar-coated caramel apple, doncha? Tsk! The kids these days.

Tip!
Try to capture the camel's main distinguishing features: its heavy-lidded eyes and hump. Also be sure to obtain a good rendition of its overall lumpy, bumpy contours.

Giraffes

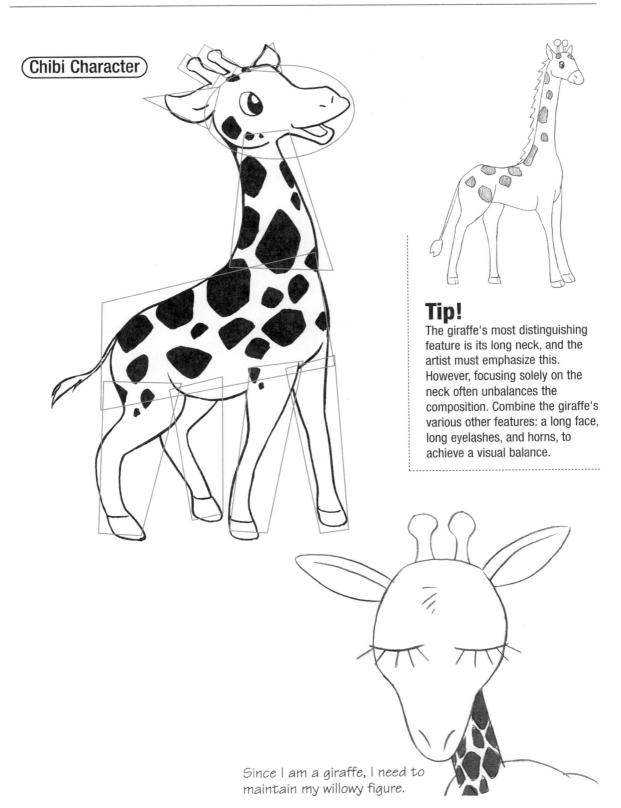

Chibi Character

Tip!
The giraffe's most distinguishing feature is its long neck, and the artist must emphasize this. However, focusing solely on the neck often unbalances the composition. Combine the giraffe's various other features: a long face, long eyelashes, and horns, to achieve a visual balance.

Since I am a giraffe, I need to maintain my willowy figure.

Gorillas

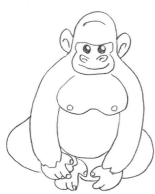

Tip!

The gorilla is a primate and making it fundamentally close to the human in form. The profile is relatively simple to capture; however, the gorilla's general beefiness and pose are also vital. This may strike you as an odd analogy, but picture a brawny middle-aged guy when drawing a gorilla. You will find it helpful in making your gorilla look convincing.

Chibi Character

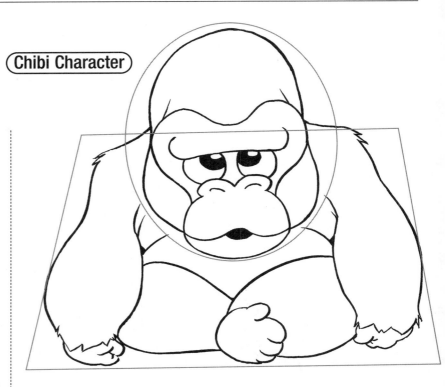

Anthropomorphized Character

Hey! I need sumptin' to drink!

Uh....What about work?

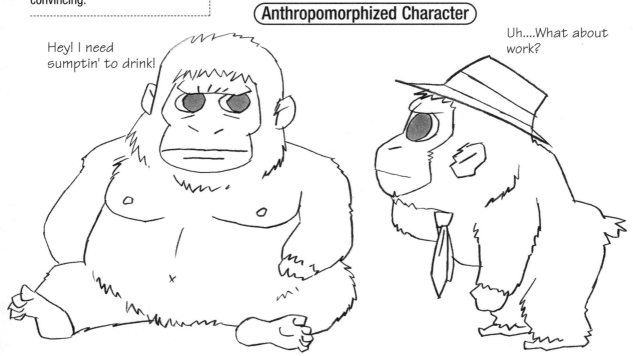

Pandas

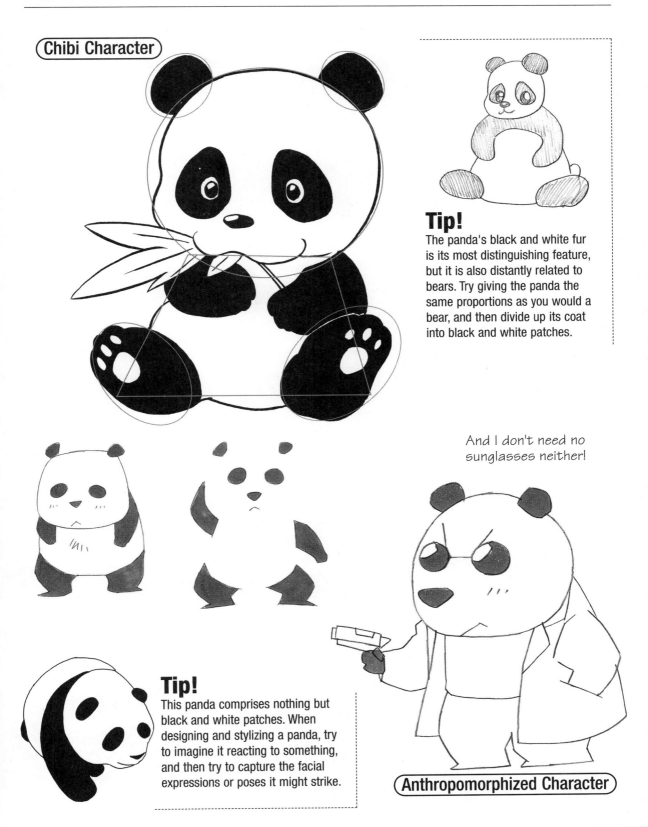

Chibi Character

Tip!
The panda's black and white fur is its most distinguishing feature, but it is also distantly related to bears. Try giving the panda the same proportions as you would a bear, and then divide up its coat into black and white patches.

And I don't need no sunglasses neither!

Tip!
This panda comprises nothing but black and white patches. When designing and stylizing a panda, try to imagine it reacting to something, and then try to capture the facial expressions or poses it might strike.

Anthropomorphized Character

Bears

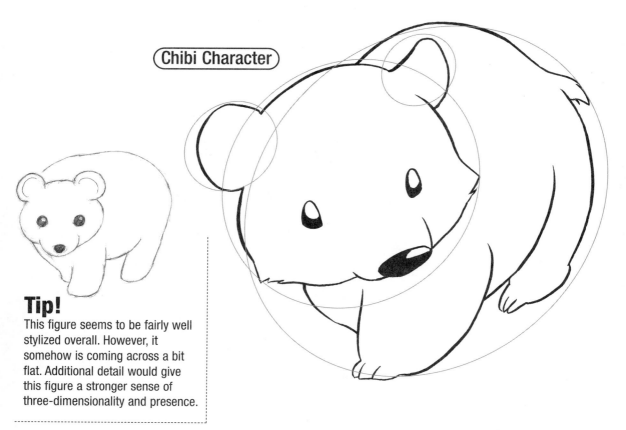

Chibi Character

Tip!
This figure seems to be fairly well stylized overall. However, it somehow is coming across a bit flat. Additional detail would give this figure a stronger sense of three-dimensionality and presence.

I'm not some souvenir from Alaska, you know.

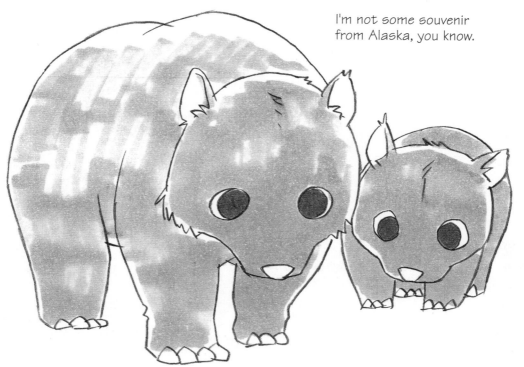

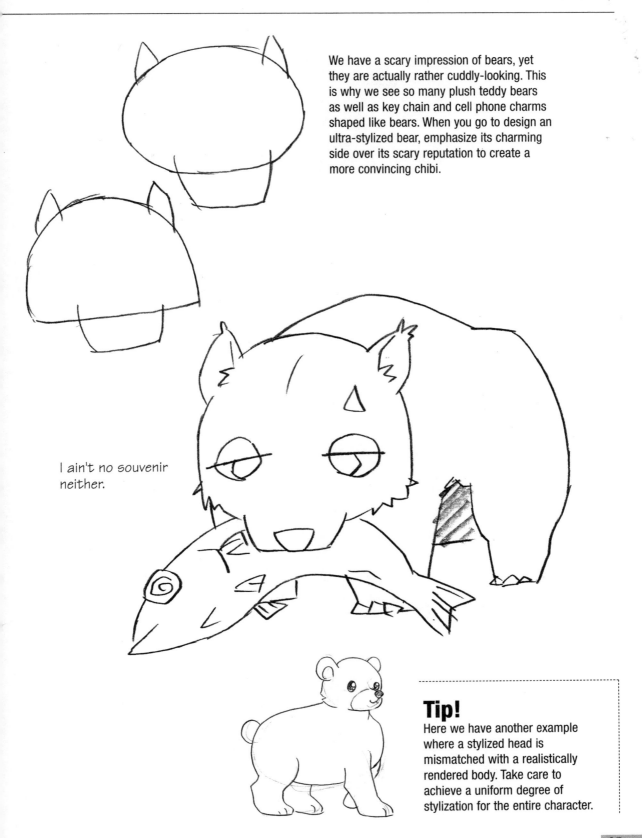

We have a scary impression of bears, yet they are actually rather cuddly-looking. This is why we see so many plush teddy bears as well as key chain and cell phone charms shaped like bears. When you go to design an ultra-stylized bear, emphasize its charming side over its scary reputation to create a more convincing chibi.

I ain't no souvenir neither.

Tip!
Here we have another example where a stylized head is mismatched with a realistically rendered body. Take care to achieve a uniform degree of stylization for the entire character.

How can I make my chibi character ferocious?

Answer

Consider for a moment what aspect of an animal gives it a sense of strength when you see it. In the case of the lion, it's fangs. In the case of a hippo, it's a huge mouth. Try exaggerating these features, adjusting their size, and using shading and highlights to emphasize them. This should add to the character's sense of dynamism.

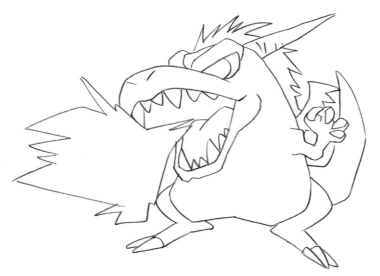

Key Points in Intensifying a Character

Whether you are drawing a dragon or a tiger, do not portray it straight on. Even tilting the head slightly completely alters the image.

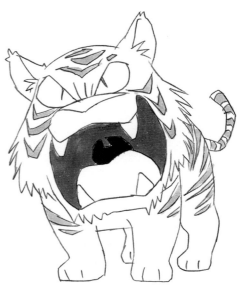

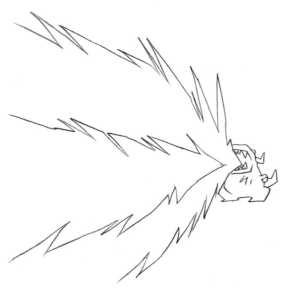

Stylize This!

Drawing the character in an exaggerated perspective sometimes can be beneficial, even if it diverges from reality. In the case of a real, non-fantastical animal, just draw the mouth open and on the large side.

All of my chibi characters seem the same. What can I do?

Answer

You seem to be experiencing troubles in imbuing your characters with distinguishing characteristics. If you are finding it difficult to capture the animals' identifying traits, take a close look at the main characters in Disney features and try to feel truly involved in the movie. The ability to feel moved by a character is based in your understanding of that character's identifying traits, so let this be the first step in learning about such traits or features. Watch about 100 works of manga and anime with hyper-stylization. Once you are able to feel enraptured by these characters, you will find the desire to exaggerate and stylize yourself.

If you still find yourself totally unable to become emotionally attached to these characters, or you continue to feel impassionate about them, then I suggest you put aside attempts to stylize animals for now, read "Volume 1: Humans," and focus on stylizing human characters.

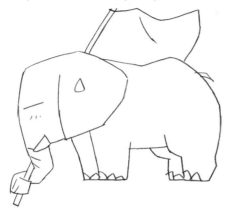

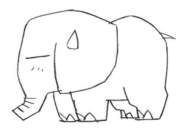

Outer differences:
Vary the characters' builds

Different levels of agility: Vary the speeds at which the characters move

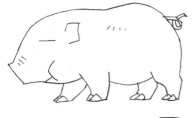 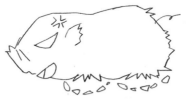 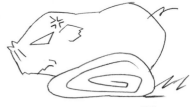

Inner differences: Vary the characters' personalities

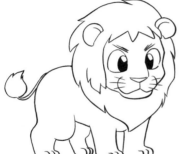

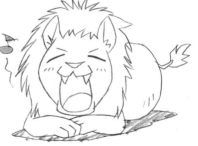

Brave Lion

Peaceful Lion

Wolves

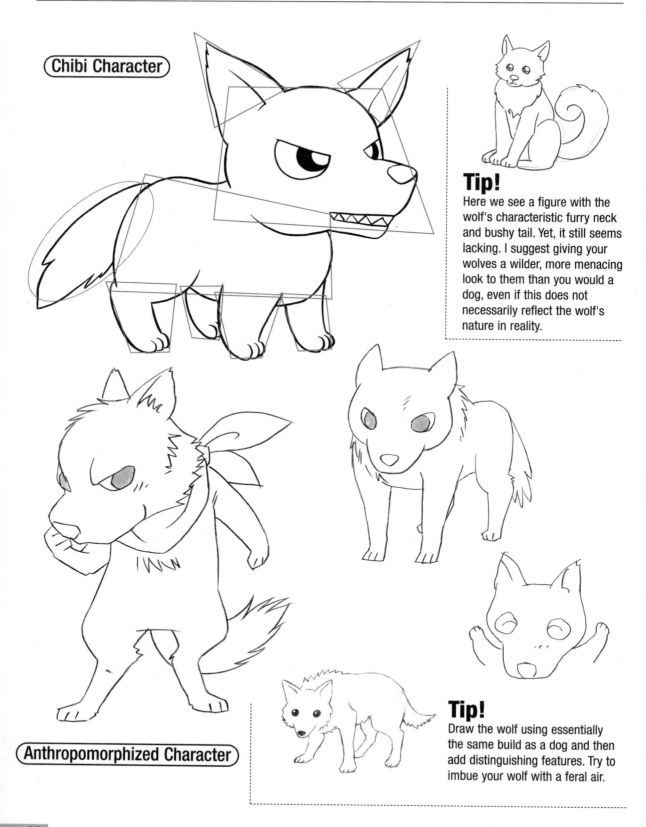

Chibi Character

Tip!
Here we see a figure with the wolf's characteristic furry neck and bushy tail. Yet, it still seems lacking. I suggest giving your wolves a wilder, more menacing look to them than you would a dog, even if this does not necessarily reflect the wolf's nature in reality.

Anthropomorphized Character

Tip!
Draw the wolf using essentially the same build as a dog and then add distinguishing features. Try to imbue your wolf with a feral air.

Kangaroos

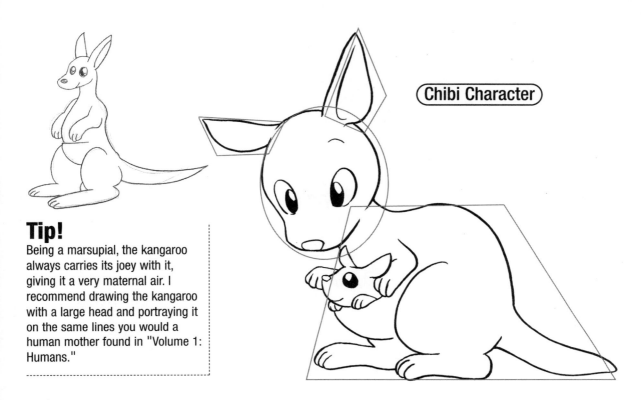

Chibi Character

Tip!

Being a marsupial, the kangaroo always carries its joey with it, giving it a very maternal air. I recommend drawing the kangaroo with a large head and portraying it on the same lines you would a human mother found in "Volume 1: Humans."

Anthropomorphized Character

What if a kangaroo turned into a person?

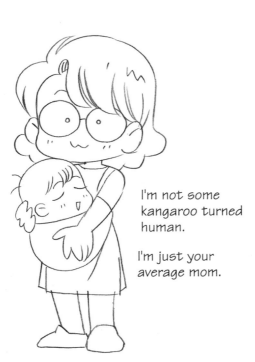

I'm not some kangaroo turned human.

I'm just your average mom.

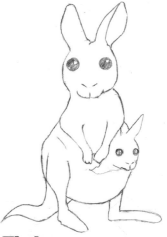

Tip!

The above figure is acceptable if you are seeking only 1st degree stylization. If you are seeking more dramatic stylization, then the distinguishing characteristics must be captured and the degree of stylization enhanced.

How should I portray furry chibi animals?

Answer

In "Volume 1: Humans," we discussed how distinguishing features of hairstyles may be defined by outlining contours of shadow. Keep in mind the degree of stylization you plan to use, and decide what will be the maximum thickness of the lines for the composition, adjusting and simplifying the fur and other details to that given thickness.

Japanese Dog: Short Fur

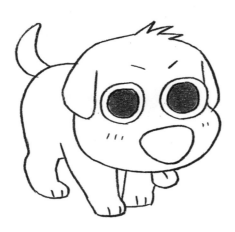

Western Dog: Long Fur

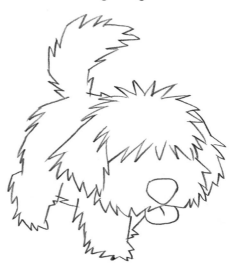

Japanese Cat: Shorthair

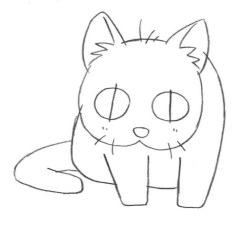

Western Cat: Longhair

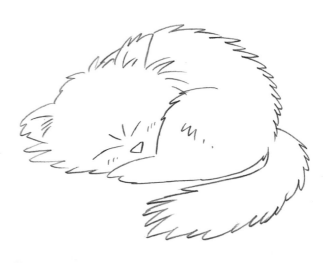

Owls

Us snowy owls
are totally white.

(Chibi Character)

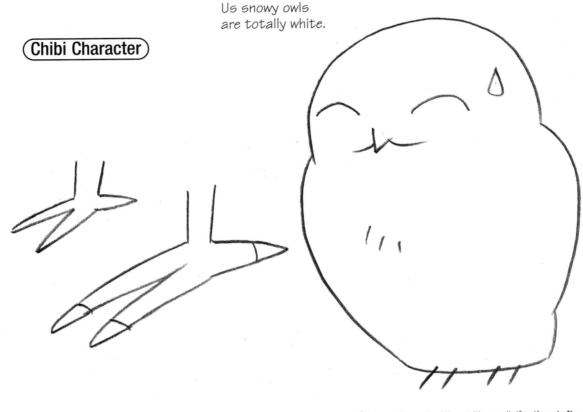

Owls with and without "horns" (feather tufts on the head) can be difficult to distinguish from one another when stylized. Maintain a basic bird form, thickening the neck, rotating the eyes to the front of the face, and draw the beak on the small side to achieve an appropriately "owlish" look. To add detailing, use abstracted symbols on the wings to represent feathers.

While this may be a bit of an exaggeration, bird claws may generally be represented using lines only, provided that they match the stylization level of the composition as a whole. However, if the bird needs to take action, then line-rendered claws may become a handicap; therefore, I recommend instead using simplified forms to portray bird claws.

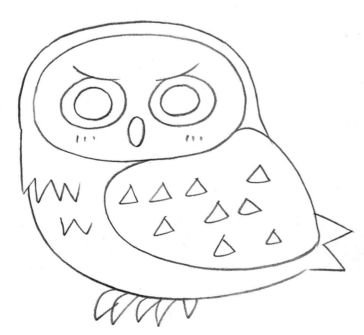

Cranes, Sparrows, and Swallows

Chibi Character

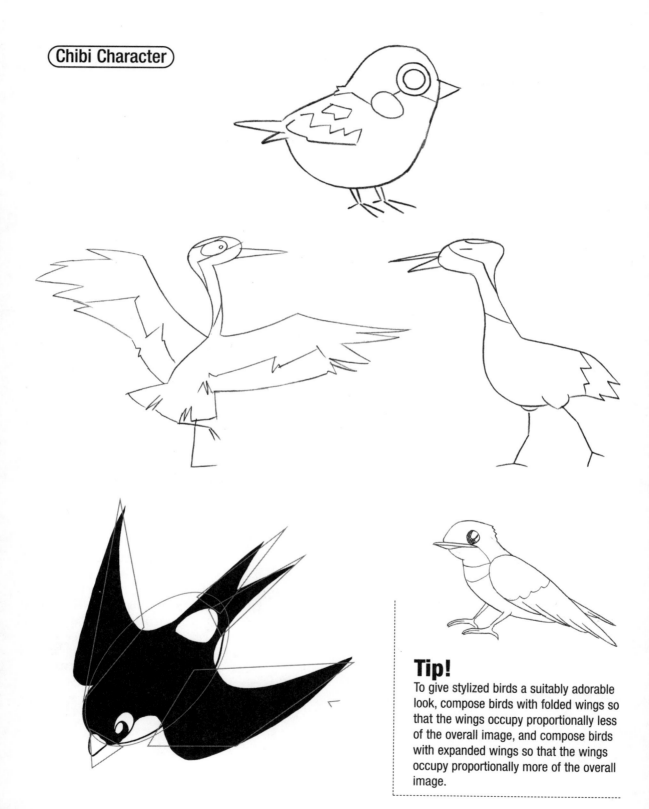

Tip!

To give stylized birds a suitably adorable look, compose birds with folded wings so that the wings occupy proportionally less of the overall image, and compose birds with expanded wings so that the wings occupy proportionally more of the overall image.

Swans

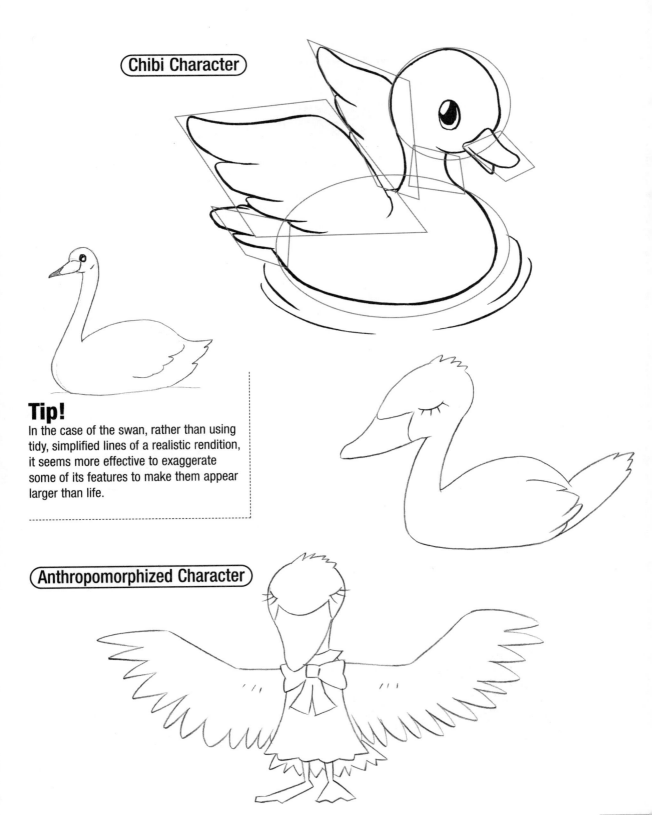

Chibi Character

Tip!
In the case of the swan, rather than using tidy, simplified lines of a realistic rendition, it seems more effective to exaggerate some of its features to make them appear larger than life.

Anthropomorphized Character

Crows

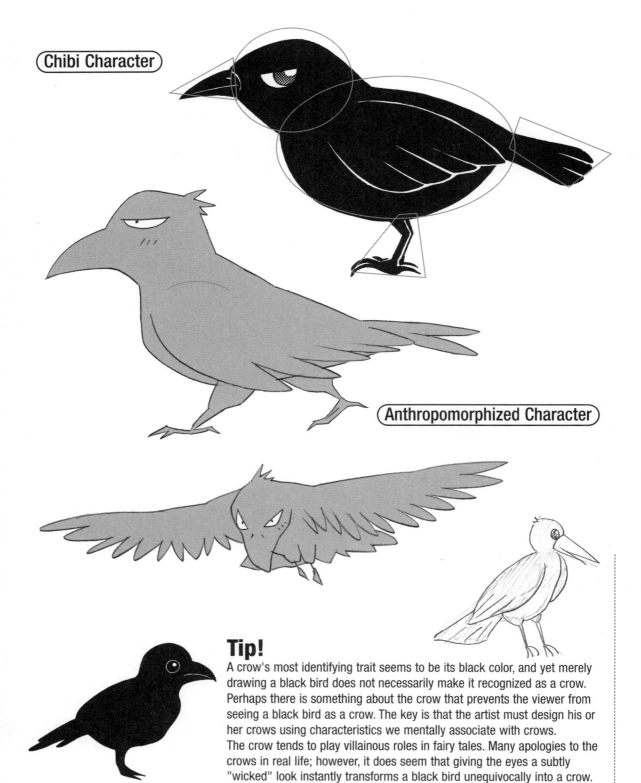

Chibi Character

Anthropomorphized Character

Tip!

A crow's most identifying trait seems to be its black color, and yet merely drawing a black bird does not necessarily make it recognized as a crow. Perhaps there is something about the crow that prevents the viewer from seeing a black bird as a crow. The key is that the artist must design his or her crows using characteristics we mentally associate with crows.

The crow tends to play villainous roles in fairy tales. Many apologies to the crows in real life; however, it does seem that giving the eyes a subtly "wicked" look instantly transforms a black bird unequivocally into a crow.

Eagles and Hawks

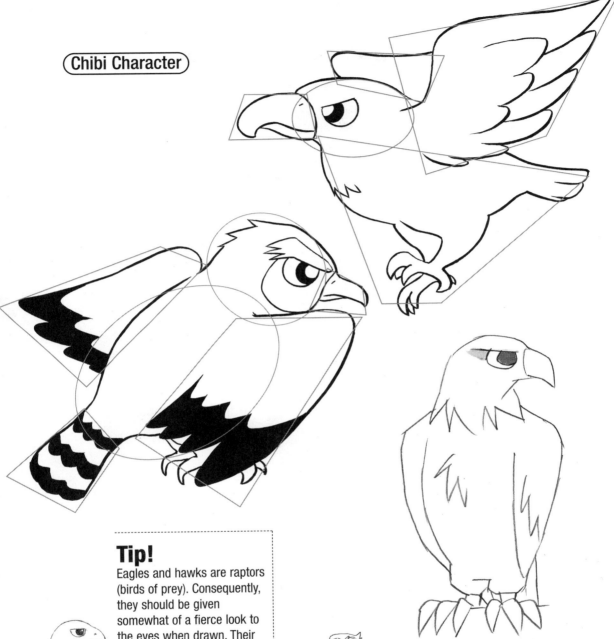

Chibi Character

Tip!
Eagles and hawks are raptors (birds of prey). Consequently, they should be given somewhat of a fierce look to the eyes when drawn. Their bodies are large, and when their wings are fully extended, they occasionally reach lengths longer than a person is tall. However, going back to the mantra I've been droning on throughout this book, emphasizing solely the body's largeness severely robs the character of its proportional balance.

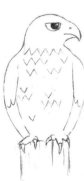

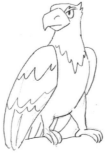

Tip!
Rather than emphasizing the length of a raptor's wingspan, it might be more effective to exaggerate instead its shoulder breadth. Next, eliminate any extraneous lines, maintaining only those that make the figure trim and streamlined, indicating potential speed.

Ducks and Geese

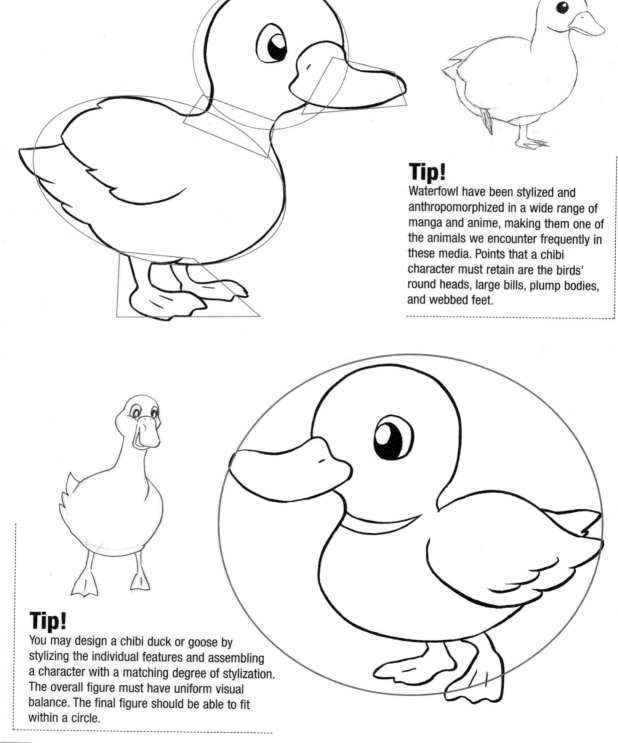

Chibi Character

Tip!
Waterfowl have been stylized and anthropomorphized in a wide range of manga and anime, making them one of the animals we encounter frequently in these media. Points that a chibi character must retain are the birds' round heads, large bills, plump bodies, and webbed feet.

Tip!
You may design a chibi duck or goose by stylizing the individual features and assembling a character with a matching degree of stylization. The overall figure must have uniform visual balance. The final figure should be able to fit within a circle.

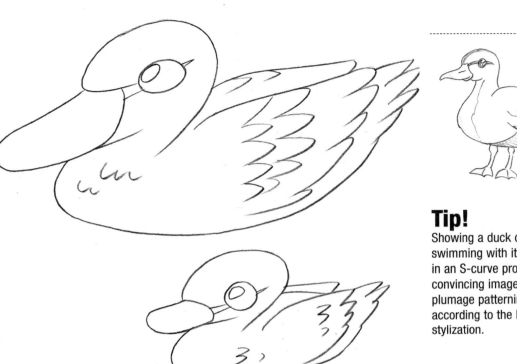

Tip!

Showing a duck or a goose swimming with its neck relaxed in an S-curve produces a convincing image. Abbreviate the plumage patterning as necessary according to the level of stylization.

(Anthropomorphized Character)

What if a duck turned into a person?

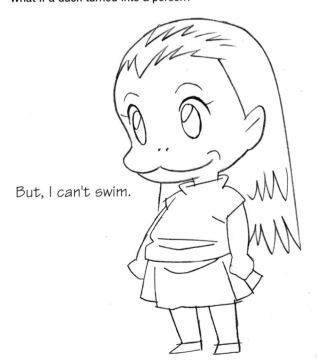

But, I can't swim.

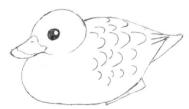

Tip!

Generally speaking, drawing birds with large heads makes them more endearing. I recommend designing the overall figure's proportions assuming that the duck will have a big head. This should facilitate the process.

Chickens

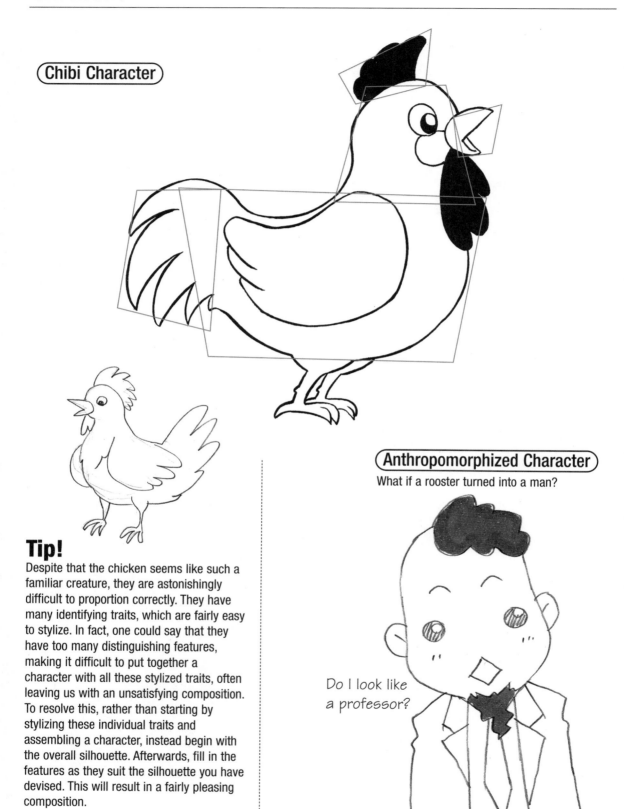

Chibi Character

Anthropomorphized Character

What if a rooster turned into a man?

Do I look like a professor?

Tip!

Despite that the chicken seems like such a familiar creature, they are astonishingly difficult to proportion correctly. They have many identifying traits, which are fairly easy to stylize. In fact, one could say that they have too many distinguishing features, making it difficult to put together a character with all these stylized traits, often leaving us with an unsatisfying composition. To resolve this, rather than starting by stylizing these individual traits and assembling a character, instead begin with the overall silhouette. Afterwards, fill in the features as they suit the silhouette you have devised. This will result in a fairly pleasing composition.

Peacocks

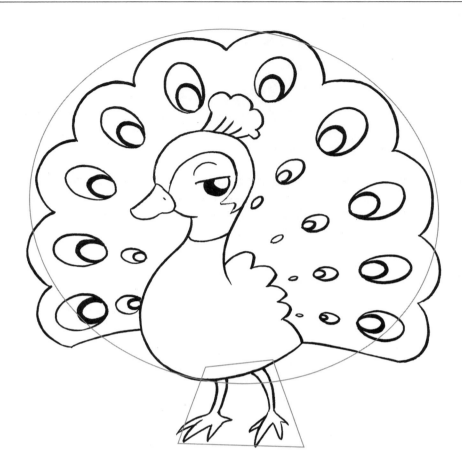

(**Anthropomorphized Character**)

What if a peacock turned into a person?

I'm not an anthropomorphization, so much as I'm a beautiful bird.

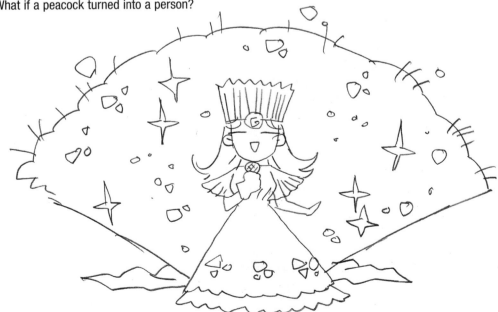

How do you draw the back of a chibi animal's head?

Answer

First of all, be sure you carefully study the animals you plan to draw. As with other views, if you are familiar with the animal's skeletal and muscular structure, you should gain an understanding of how the bones and muscles work when the animal turns its head and looks back.

Take extra care with how you proportion a chibi animal's ears, as they constitute a key element in achieving a pleasing composition. I suggest you ask others to look at your work. As I have been trying to hammer home throughout this book, in order to ensure that the character elicits parental instincts in the viewer, merely showing your artwork to a variety of people and asking their opinions will help you learn to design an appealing composition.

Always Maintain a Three-Dimensional Image of the Character

Front
The feature you should note when looking at a character from the front is the triangle formed by the eyes and the nose. Be sure you have this positioning down well. The same holds true for human figures.

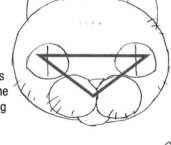

Back
The rear of the head is not just fur. Visualize the face on the other side as you draw the back. In the case of vertebrates, be sure you are also familiar with skeletal connections.

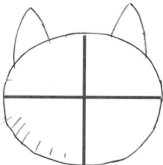

Profile
Note in the profile the line connecting the ears, eye, and nose. Conceive of this line as connecting the head to the neck.

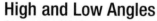

High and Low Angles
As mentioned above, you should have about half of the hurdles covered if you have a firm grasp of the physical relationship between all those parts or features connected to the head. The remaining hurdles to overcome are how to visualize and conceive of these various features as solid objects.

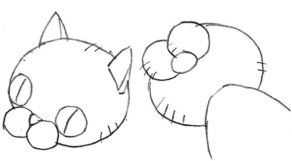

Porpoises

Chibi Character

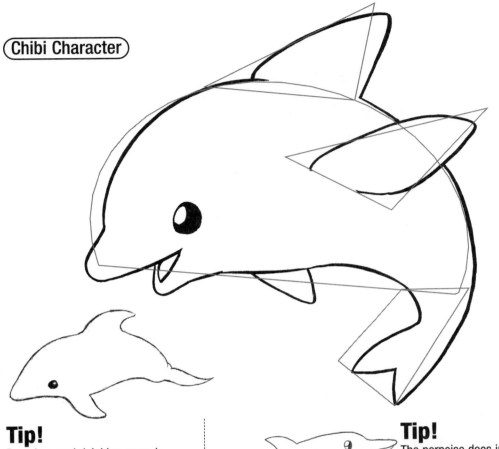

Tip!

Porpoises and dolphins seem to appear quite frequently as characters, suggesting that we feel attached to them in an amicable, friendly way. Therefore, I recommend using clearly defined facial expressions on porpoise characters.

Tip!

The porpoise does indeed have a long mouth. However, if all you do is make the mouth long, an awkward-looking character will result. Study the animal's skeletal structure before fleshing it out.

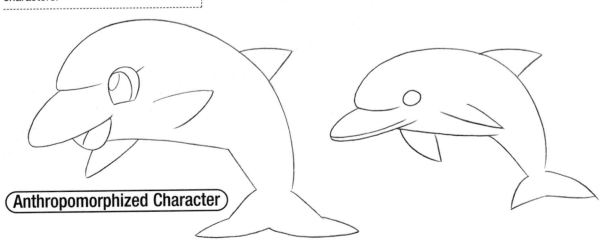

Anthropomorphized Character

Whales and Orcas

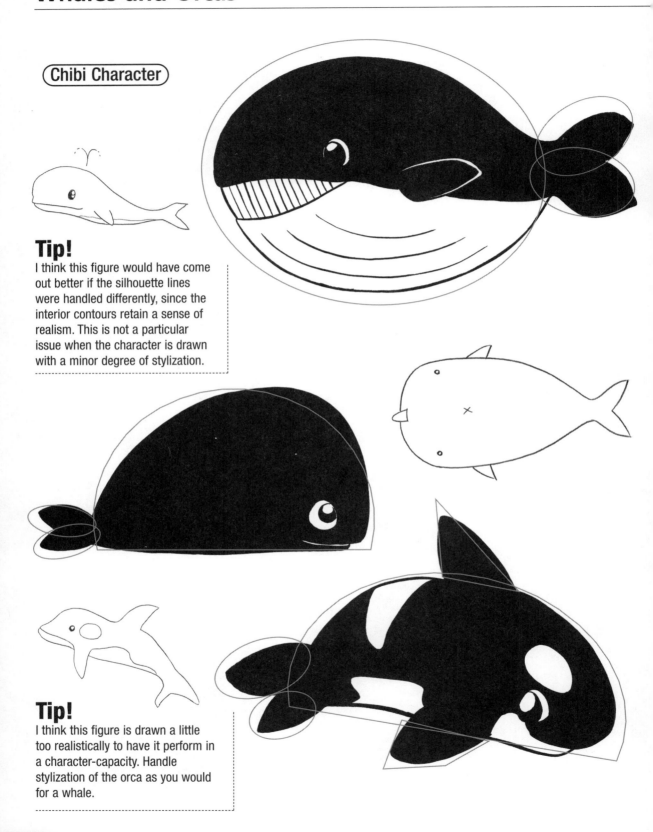

Chibi Character

Tip!
I think this figure would have come out better if the silhouette lines were handled differently, since the interior contours retain a sense of realism. This is not a particular issue when the character is drawn with a minor degree of stylization.

Tip!
I think this figure is drawn a little too realistically to have it perform in a character-capacity. Handle stylization of the orca as you would for a whale.

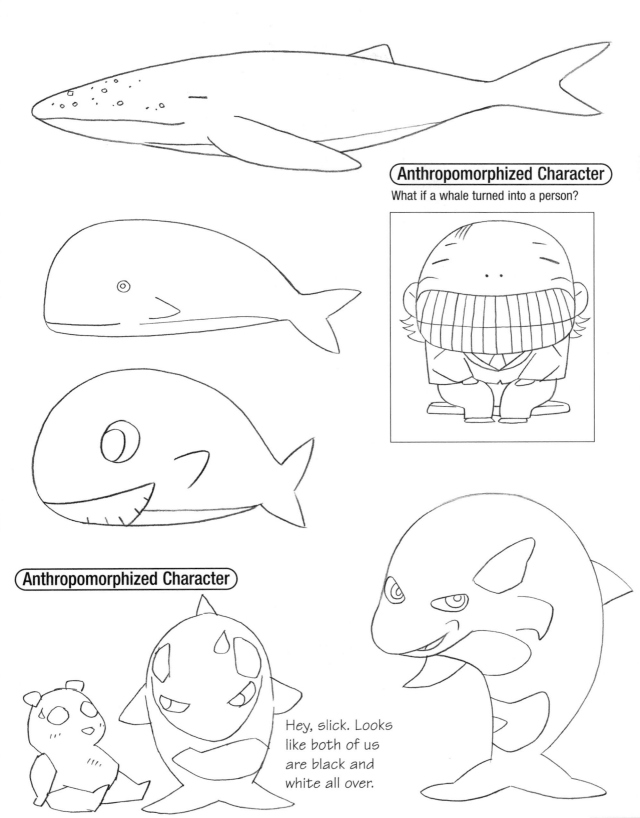

Anthropomorphized Character

What if a whale turned into a person?

Anthropomorphized Character

Hey, slick. Looks like both of us are black and white all over.

Penguins

Chibi Character

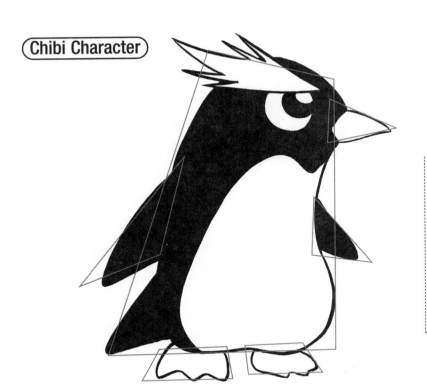

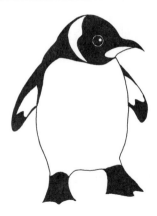

Tip!

We encounter various penguin species in the form of stylized characters. When having the character perform a role, pay attention to how you stylize its individual features.

Anthropomorphized Character

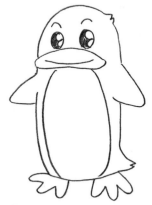

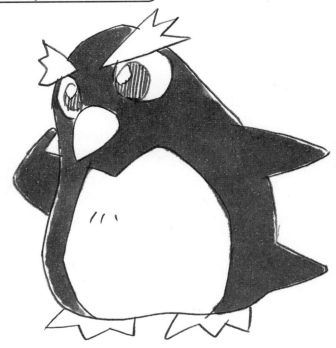

Tip!

This is a very manga-esque drawing, and it really appeals to me, personally speaking. However, the general form has been overly simplified, and the character looks a little too much like a guy in a penguin suit. I recommend selecting more animalistic, natural forms.

84

Tuna and Sharks

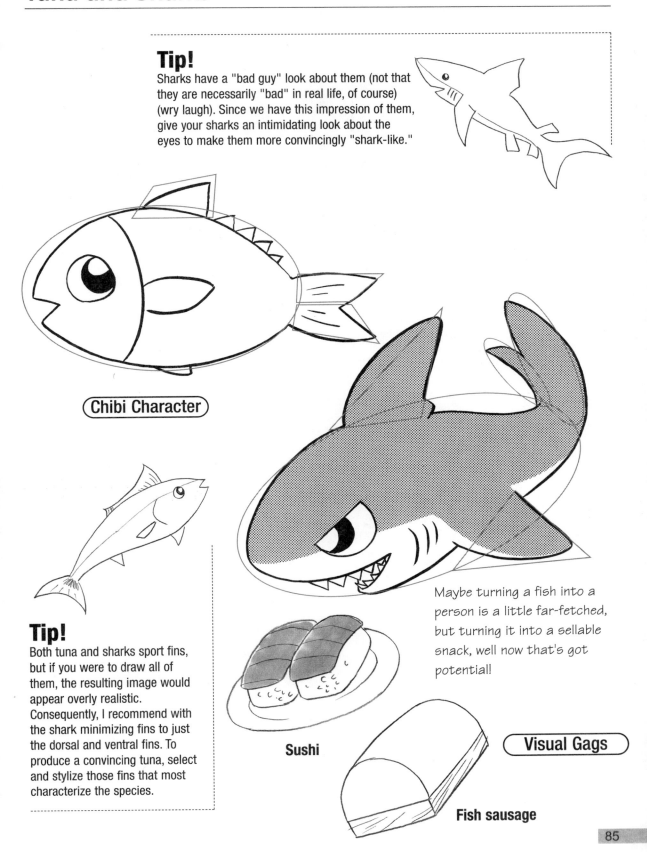

Tip!
Sharks have a "bad guy" look about them (not that they are necessarily "bad" in real life, of course) (wry laugh). Since we have this impression of them, give your sharks an intimidating look about the eyes to make them more convincingly "shark-like."

Chibi Character

Tip!
Both tuna and sharks sport fins, but if you were to draw all of them, the resulting image would appear overly realistic. Consequently, I recommend with the shark minimizing fins to just the dorsal and ventral fins. To produce a convincing tuna, select and stylize those fins that most characterize the species.

Maybe turning a fish into a person is a little far-fetched, but turning it into a sellable snack, well now that's got potential!

Sushi

Visual Gags

Fish sausage

Octopuses

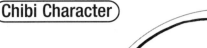

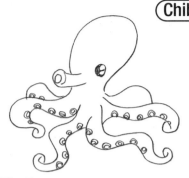

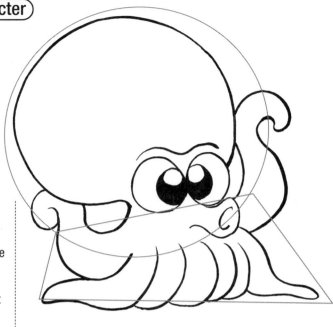

Tip!

Octopuses' eyes, mouths, and other features are actually not constructed in a way that lends itself readily to transformation into a character. Consequently, it is sometimes easier visually for the viewer if the octopus has been reconstructed to look more like a human when having it perform a role. In the figure above, the legs seem to have not been stylized as much as the rest of the octopus. Take extra care when stylizing octopus parts.

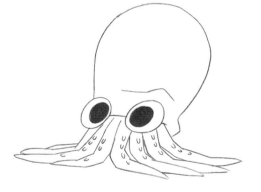

Anthropomorphized Character

What if an octopus turned into a person?

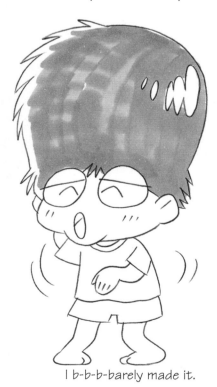

Anthropomorphized Character

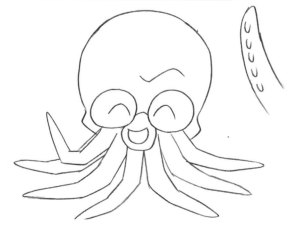

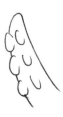

I b-b-b-barely made it.

Squids

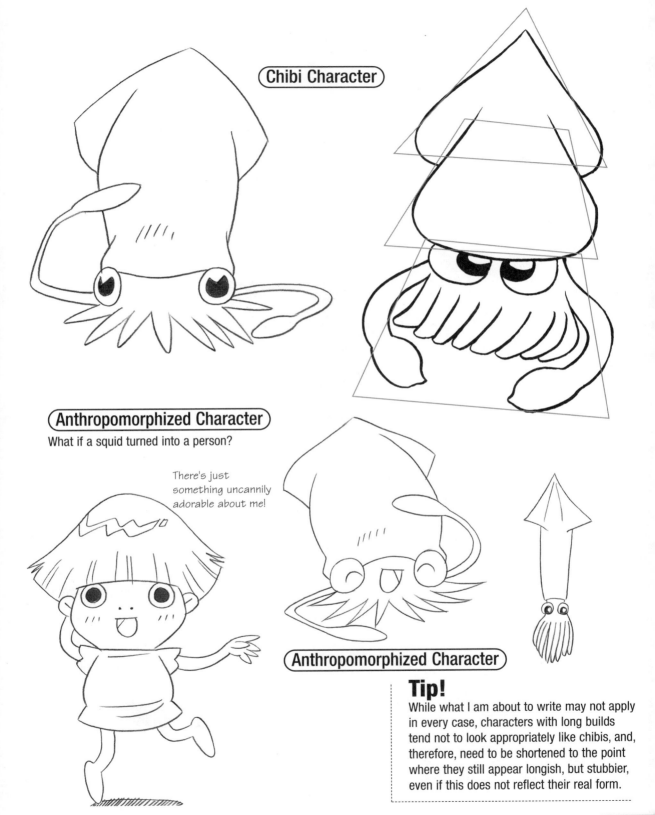

Chibi Character

Anthropomorphized Character

What if a squid turned into a person?

There's just something uncannily adorable about me!

Anthropomorphized Character

Tip!

While what I am about to write may not apply in every case, characters with long builds tend not to look appropriately like chibis, and, therefore, need to be shortened to the point where they still appear longish, but stubbier, even if this does not reflect their real form.

Mollusks

Chibi Character

Mollusk shells often display
intricate patterning, bumps,
and undulations. If the shell is
faithfully copied without
modification, it may strike us
as unattractive. Therefore, I
recommend selecting and
stylizing those bumps and
protrusions that seem
indispensable.

When having a snail, etc. play a
role, give it a face, hands, feet,
and other human features to
facilitate portrayal of emotions.
There are various modes of
adding a face; select the form
that feels the easiest to you in
making the character act.

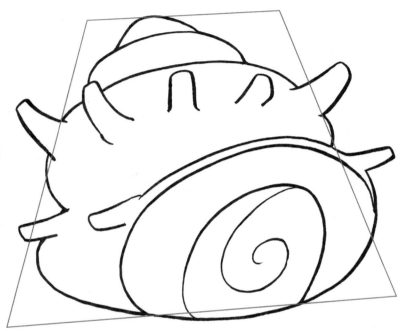

Anthropomorphized Character

What if a snail turned into a person?

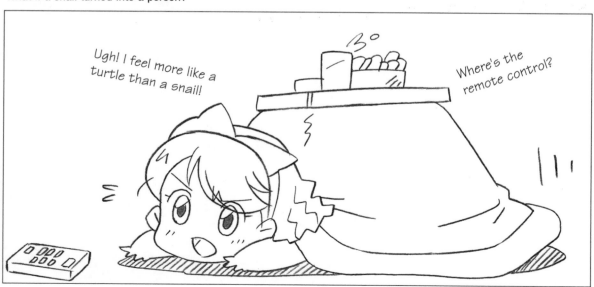

Anthropomorphized Character

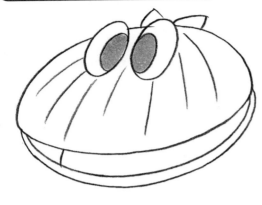

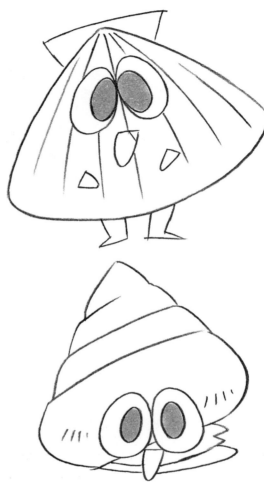

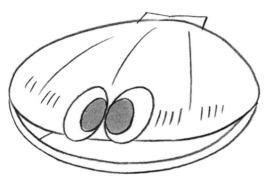

Anthropomorphized Character

What if a scallop turned into a person?

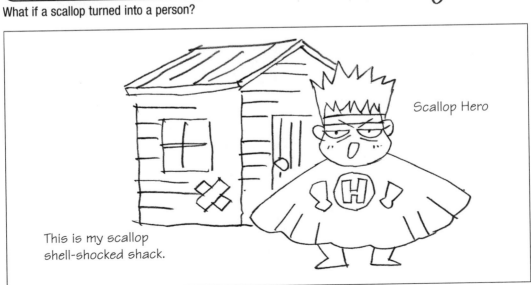

Scallop Hero

This is my scallop
shell-shocked shack.

Shrimp and Jellyfish

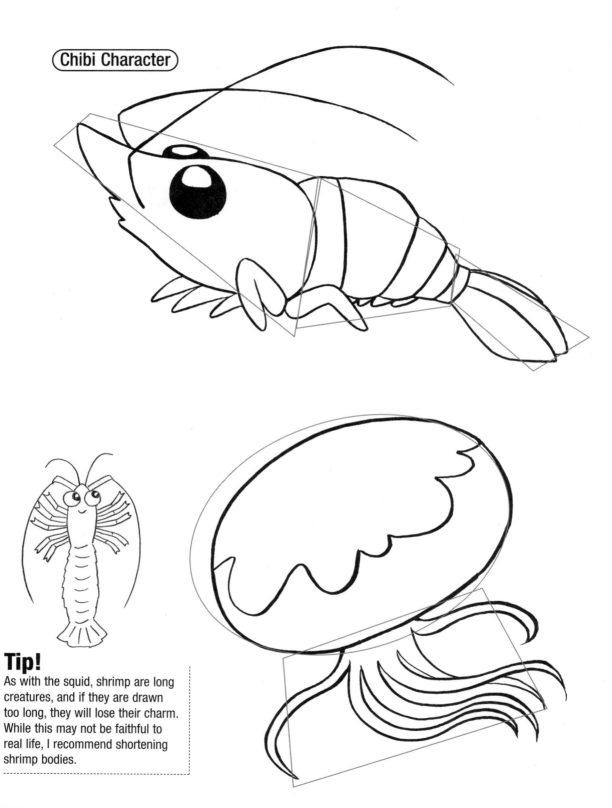

Chibi Character

Tip!
As with the squid, shrimp are long creatures, and if they are drawn too long, they will lose their charm. While this may not be faithful to real life, I recommend shortening shrimp bodies.

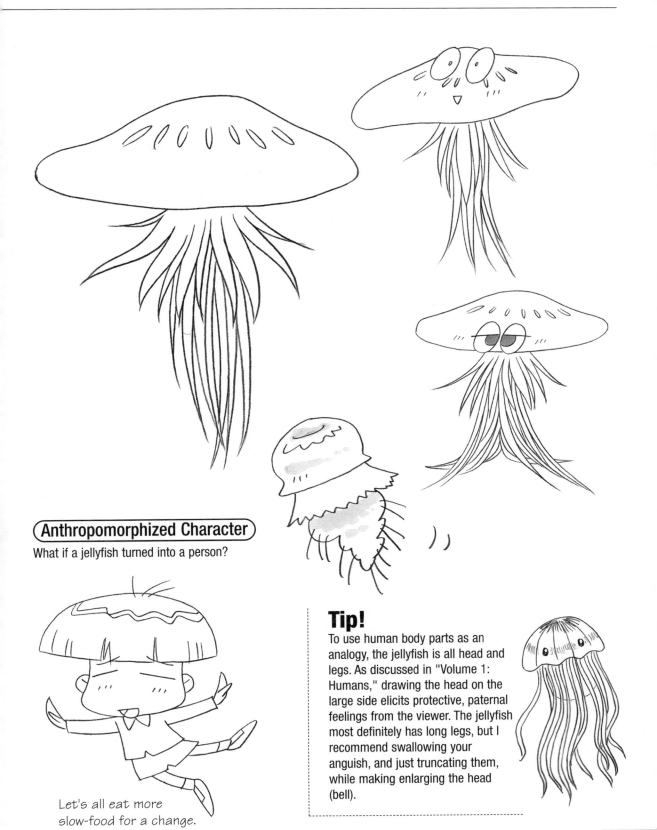

Anthropomorphized Character

What if a jellyfish turned into a person?

Let's all eat more
slow-food for a change.

Tip!

To use human body parts as an
analogy, the jellyfish is all head and
legs. As discussed in "Volume 1:
Humans," drawing the head on the
large side elicits protective, paternal
feelings from the viewer. The jellyfish
most definitely has long legs, but I
recommend swallowing your
anguish, and just truncating them,
while making enlarging the head
(bell).

I want my chibi characters to display a variety of emotions. What should I do?

Answer

When portraying emotional states, conceive of your chibi animals the same as you would chibi humans. However, you will need to familiarize yourself with the musculature involved with creating such facial expressions in order to accomplish this. You will find giving animals facial expressions an onerous task if you do not have a grasp of which muscles move and how they move to create the expression. Animals do not have what truly constitutes eyebrows. However, we can go as far to say that facial expressions may be portrayed in a general sense using the eyes and mouth. I highly recommend studying muscle and skeletal structure in earnest; it should allow you to portray facial expressions on animals as well as exaggerate them.

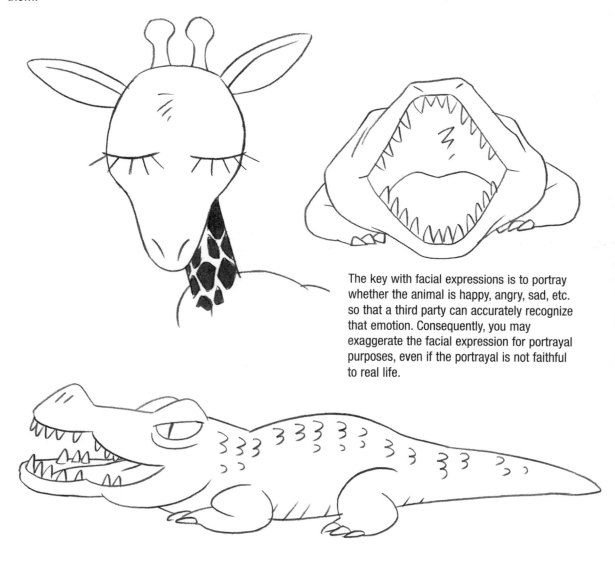

The key with facial expressions is to portray whether the animal is happy, angry, sad, etc. so that a third party can accurately recognize that emotion. Consequently, you may exaggerate the facial expression for portrayal purposes, even if the portrayal is not faithful to real life.

How can I make my chibi characters creepy?

Answer

What do you personally find disturbing or nasty? If you cannot answer this question yourself, then there is no way you are going to be able to make your characters creepy. Does the animal's feet bother you? The eyes? The tongue? Once you have identified what you find hair-raising, accentuate it using shadow, highlights, and other methods like those you would also use to enhance the ferocity of an animal.

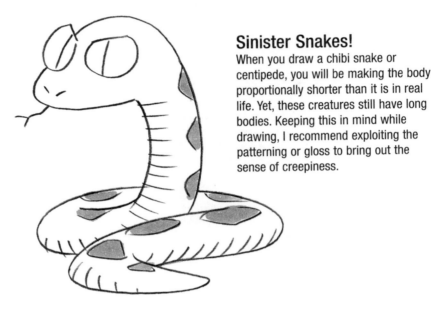

Sinister Snakes!

When you draw a chibi snake or centipede, you will be making the body proportionally shorter than it is in real life. Yet, these creatures still have long bodies. Keeping this in mind while drawing, I recommend exploiting the patterning or gloss to bring out the sense of creepiness.

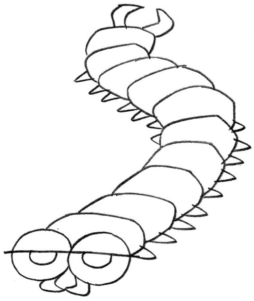

Gruesome Centipedes!

What do you find the most repugnant when you look at a centipede? If it is because the centipede has so many feet, then you will still be able to make your chibi centipede sufficiently creepy if you portray this many-legged aspect, even though the number of legs will actually be condensed. Furthermore, in consideration of people's perceptions, I suggest giving the centipede a slightly sinister look about the eyes as well.

Snakes

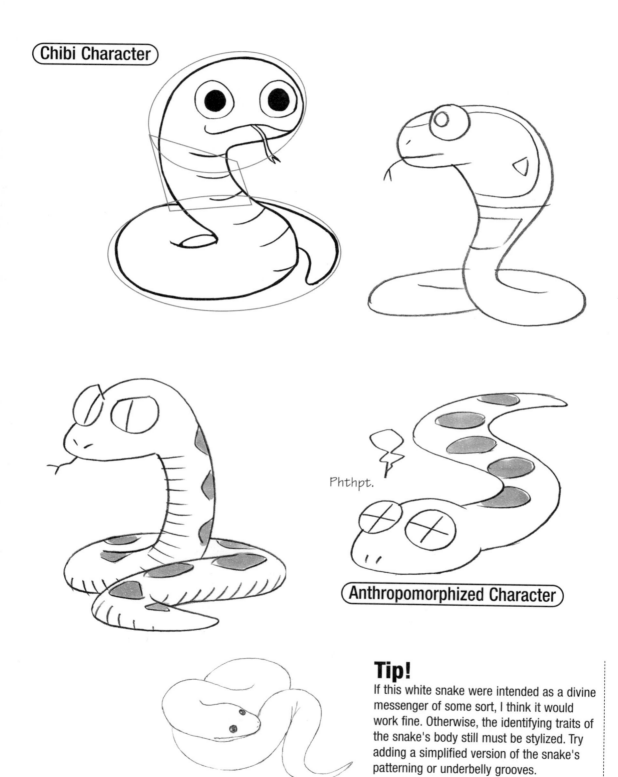

Chibi Character

Phthpt.

Anthropomorphized Character

Tip!

If this white snake were intended as a divine messenger of some sort, I think it would work fine. Otherwise, the identifying traits of the snake's body still must be stylized. Try adding a simplified version of the snake's patterning or underbelly grooves.

Frogs

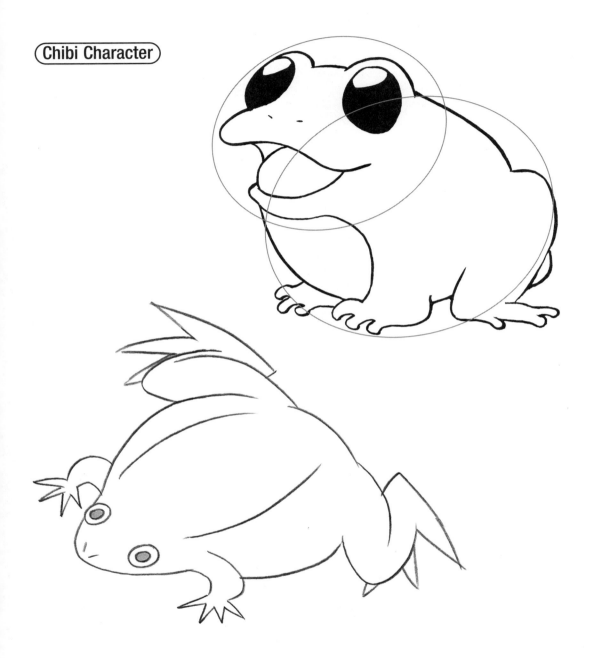

Tip!

The frog has made frequent appearances in manga since its early days. To create a frog with a generous range of facial expressions, give it a human mouth and eyes, enlarge the head, and make sure you have proportioned the figure appropriately.

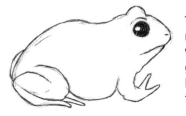

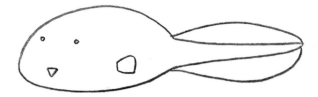

Tadpoles of Varying Degrees of Stylization

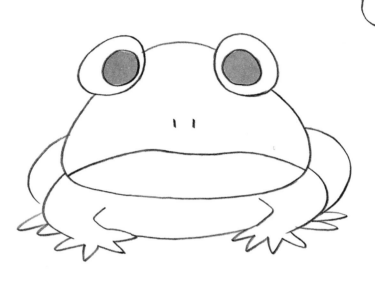

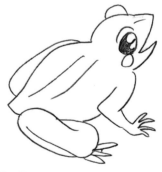

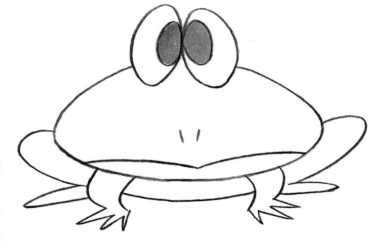

Tip!
This figure's head has been satisfyingly stylized, but I suggest making the body a smidgen smaller to achieve a pleasing visual balance. In contrast, the legs are too long. Shortening them a bit will make this character more endearing.

Iguanas

Chibi Character

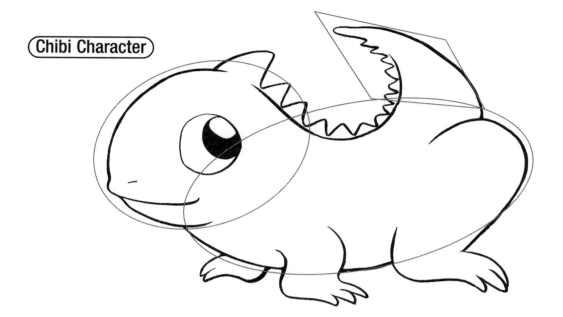

Anthropomorphized Character

What if an iguana turned into a person?

Now, isn't she pretty for someone who grew up in a burrow?

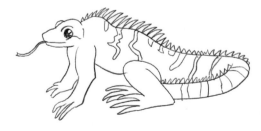

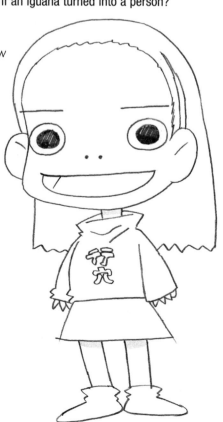

Tip!
The figure has a tremendously small head, doesn't it? I think the stylization of the head has been well handled here but would like to see the lumps and undulations of the body abbreviated a bit more.

Geckos and Salamanders

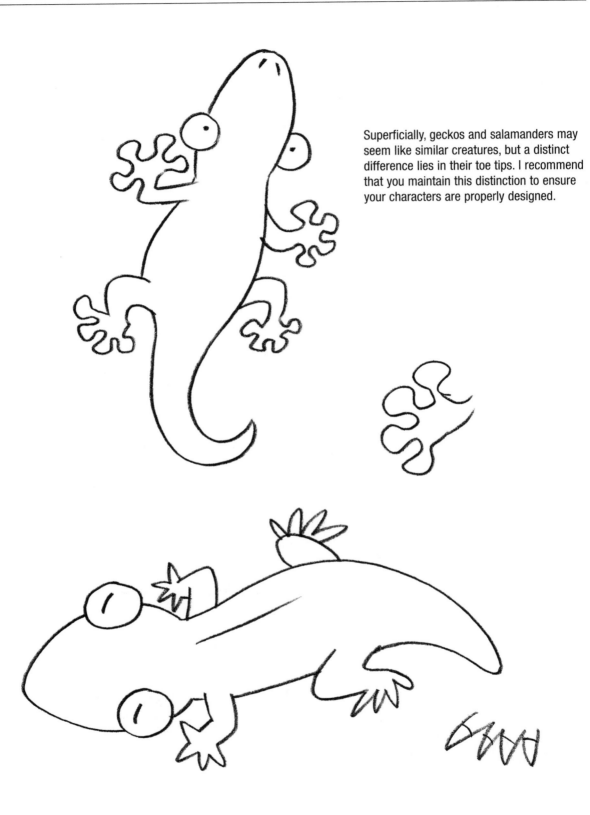

Superficially, geckos and salamanders may seem like similar creatures, but a distinct difference lies in their toe tips. I recommend that you maintain this distinction to ensure your characters are properly designed.

Turtles

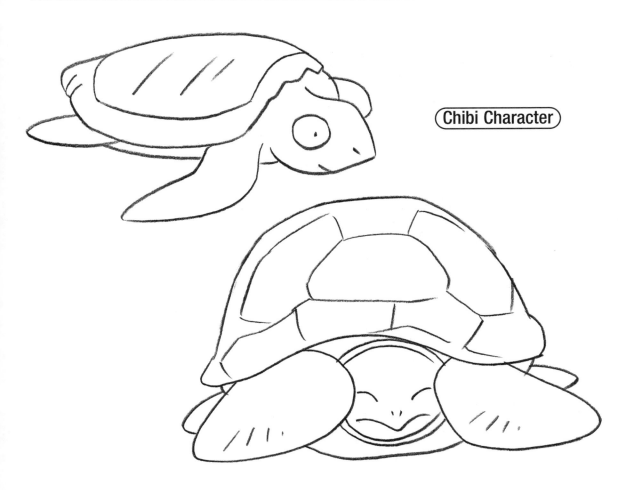

Chibi Character

Anthropomorphized Character

What if a turtle turned into a person?

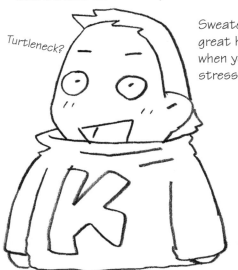

Turtleneck?

Sweaters make great hidey-holes when you're feeling stressed out.

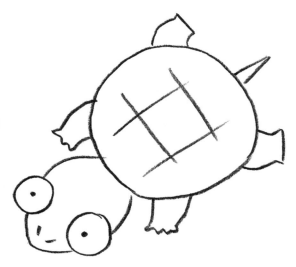

One of the ways a character's individuality can be evoked is to show the eyes protruding from the head's silhouette.

Chameleons

Chibi Character

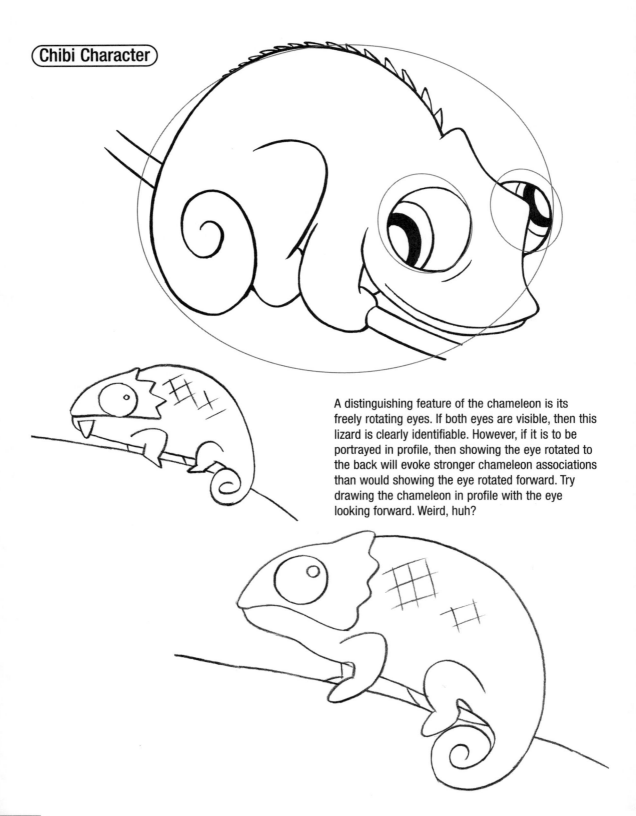

A distinguishing feature of the chameleon is its freely rotating eyes. If both eyes are visible, then this lizard is clearly identifiable. However, if it is to be portrayed in profile, then showing the eye rotated to the back will evoke stronger chameleon associations than would showing the eye rotated forward. Try drawing the chameleon in profile with the eye looking forward. Weird, huh?

Bats and Grasshoppers

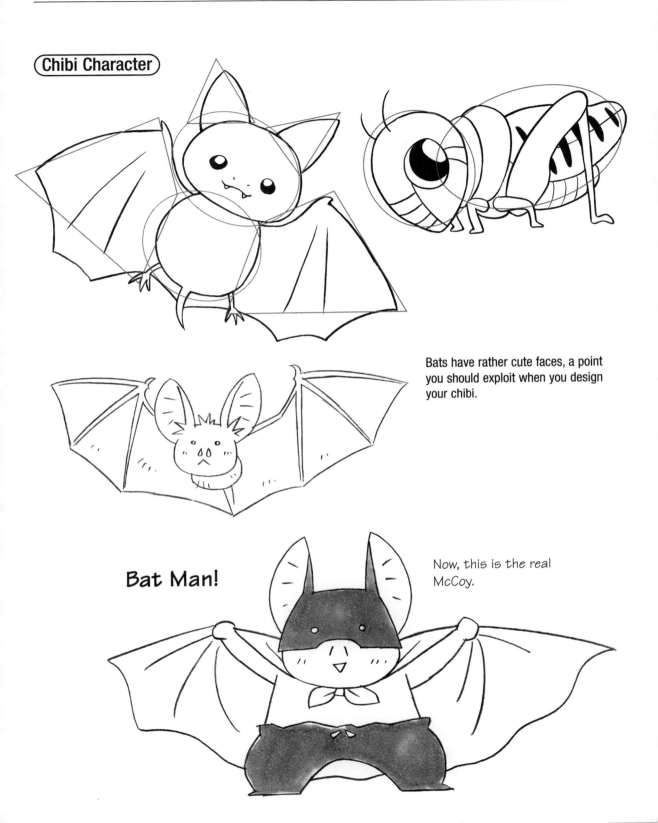

Chibi Character

Bats have rather cute faces, a point you should exploit when you design your chibi.

Bat Man!

Now, this is the real McCoy.

Beetles, Scorpions, and Cockroaches

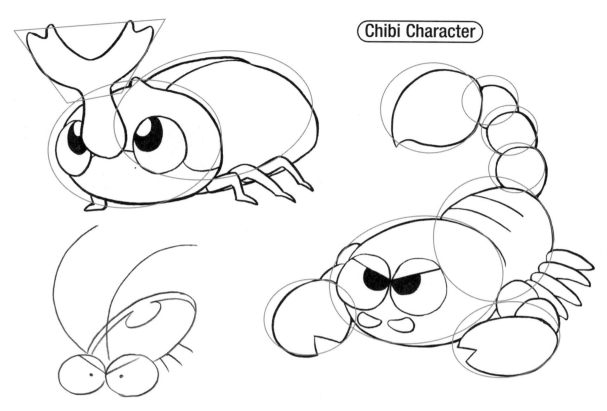

Chibi Character

When drawing bugs of any kind, it is critical that you maintain smallish forms. The character should not seem big or long. They should seem like they could fit easily into one of those plastic eggs you find in bubblegum machines.

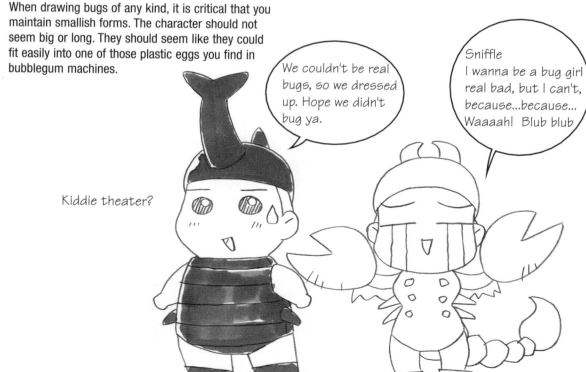

Kiddie theater?

We couldn't be real bugs, so we dressed up. Hope we didn't bug ya.

Sniffle
I wanna be a bug girl real bad, but I can't, because...because... Waaaah! Blub blub

Dragons

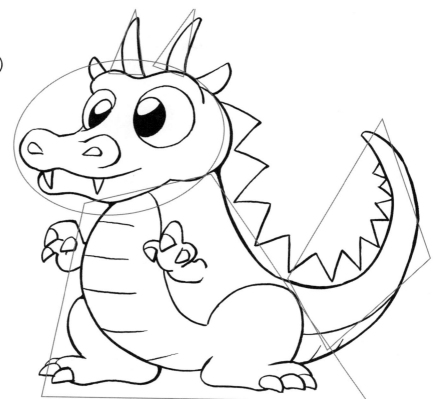

Chibi Character

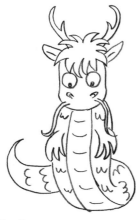

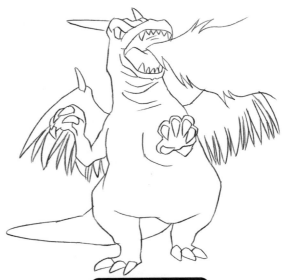

Incorrect Examples

Tip!

Dragons are mythical creatures, so they have no proper and correct form, other than designing them in a "convincing" fashion. Therefore, in the case of the figure above, I suggest making the horns more prominent, since horns and scales are strong dragon features. In addition, too many scales make the character look fussy. Eliminating some of them could alleviate this.

Needless to say, the head and body proportioning on this figure are off. It also has too many horns. This figure is chock-o-block full of lines that should have been omitted.

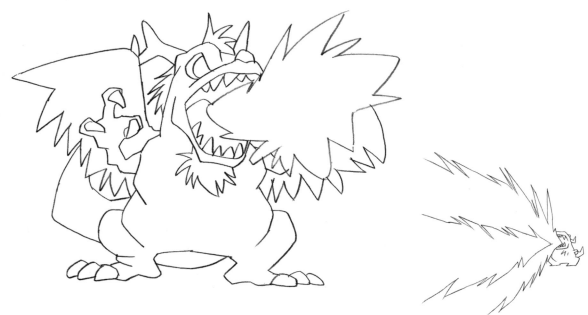

Rather than showing your dragon spew flames with
its neck straight, tilt the head a tad for a more
convincing look. There are dragons that blast out
frozen breath, so try playing around with various
character designs.

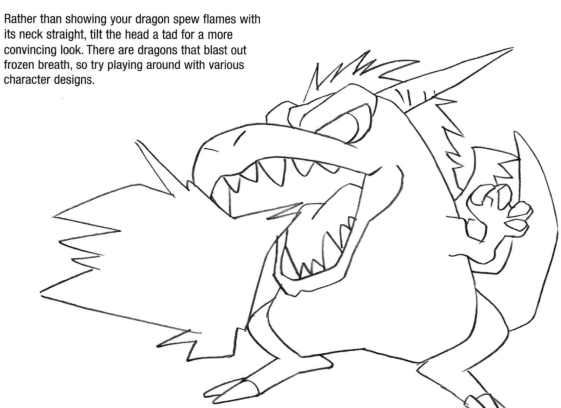

Dinosaurs

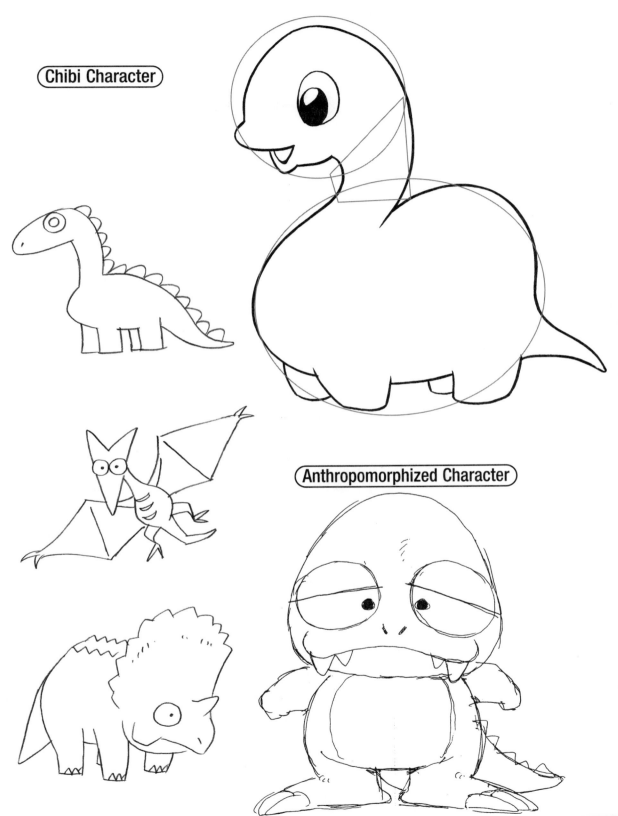

Chibi Character

Anthropomorphized Character

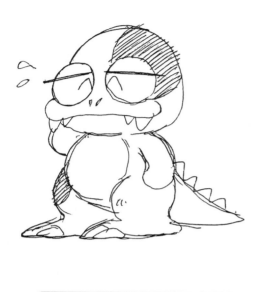

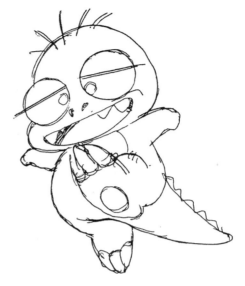

Anthropomorphized Character

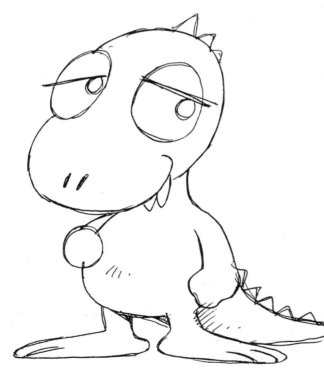

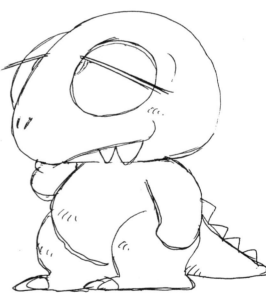

What you see on this page are all rough sketches of an anthropomorphized character I created for a project. Feel free to use them as reference in creating your own designs.

Unicorns, Pegasus, and the Phoenix

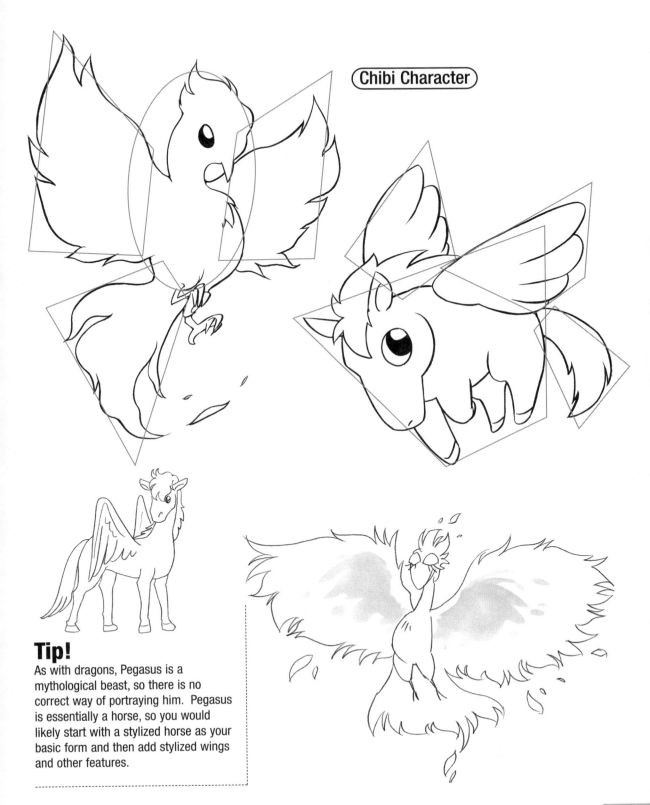

Chibi Character

Tip!
As with dragons, Pegasus is a mythological beast, so there is no correct way of portraying him. Pegasus is essentially a horse, so you would likely start with a stylized horse as your basic form and then add stylized wings and other features.

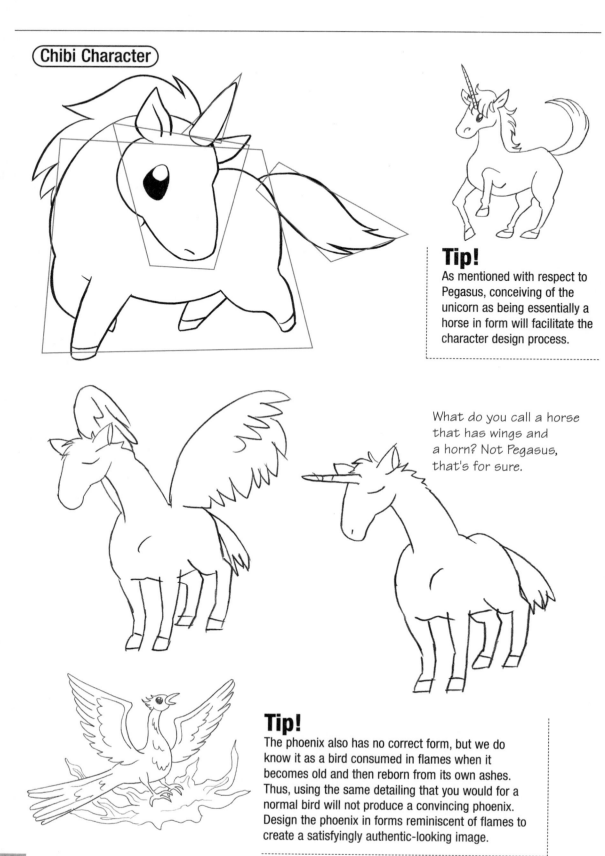

Chibi Character

Tip!
As mentioned with respect to Pegasus, conceiving of the unicorn as being essentially a horse in form will facilitate the character design process.

What do you call a horse that has wings and a horn? Not Pegasus, that's for sure.

Tip!
The phoenix also has no correct form, but we do know it as a bird consumed in flames when it becomes old and then reborn from its own ashes. Thus, using the same detailing that you would for a normal bird will not produce a convincing phoenix. Design the phoenix in forms reminiscent of flames to create a satisfyingly authentic-looking image.

What should I do to turn mythical beasts into chibi characters?

Answer

Handle mythical creatures the same as you would real animals. Provided you have identified their distinguishing characteristics, this should be an easy task. Many people wonder what real-life animal would be best to use as a model for Pegasus, dragons, and other imaginary animals, since they appear in a variety of forms depending on the example artwork selected. However, these are ultimately make-believe beasts that have no correct form. Consequently, you should base your design on whatever aspects you feel best identify the creature.

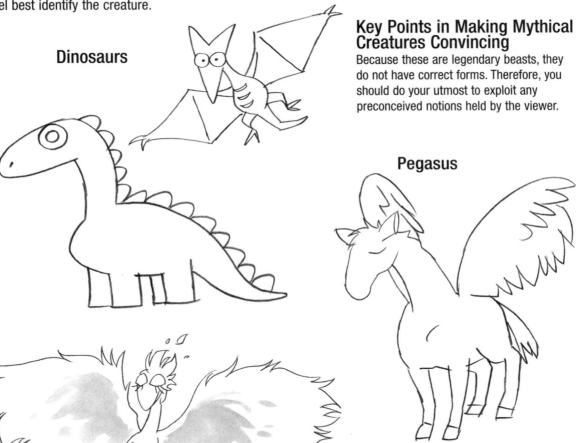

Dinosaurs

Pegasus

The Phoenix

Key Points in Making Mythical Creatures Convincing

Because these are legendary beasts, they do not have correct forms. Therefore, you should do your utmost to exploit any preconceived notions held by the viewer.

Key Points in Making Mythical Creatures Convincing

I highly recommend identifying those features that distinguish the animal and exploiting these features when designing the character. This will help the viewer recognize the creature and will draw out the character's individuality.

Game Illustration Gallery

The following pages introduce various game characters I designed. I created these characters over ten years ago, so they strike me as somewhat amateurish when I look at them now, but it would please me greatly if you are still able to use them as reference.

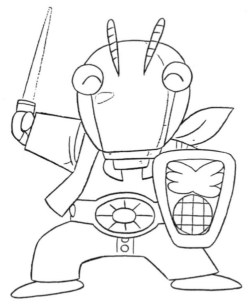

Grasshopper Mask

This character is a grasshopper and human hybrid. I bet that sounds pretty convoluted, doesn't it? (Smirk) The belt is fussy-looking as well. The shield motif is supposed to be a bird flying over the world. I bet only the old geezer readers picked up on that one. (Wry smile)

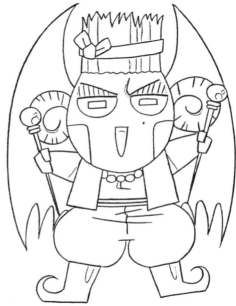

Demon Hell Master

I designed this combination of demonic features—ram horns, eyes, and bat wings—when a certain rock band was popular in Japan.

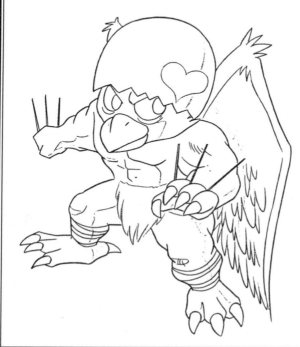

Muscle Chicken

In some English-speaking countries, to be "chicken" means you're a coward, so I thought I might take the plunge and create a strong chicken. Notice that he is armed with chicken shish kabob-style bamboo skewers to pierce his enemies.

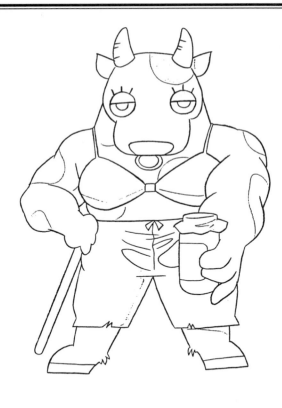

Milk Wonder

As with Muscle Chicken, I thought I would create an incongruent character, in this case milk coming from a burly cow—and, who could refuse? (Grin)

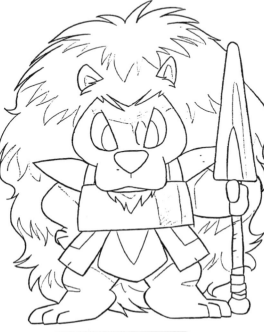

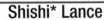

Shishi* Lance

As you can see, this character was based on a lion. Compared with the other work I produced during this period, he strikes me as a tightly pulled together character.
*Mythical Chinese lion

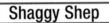

Shaggy Shep

Here we see a shaggy sheepdog in full knight garb. He's one of those characters where we can't tell if he's tough or wimpy just by looking. (Wry smile) I drew his leg joints and other body parts as if he were human to show him standing upright like a person.

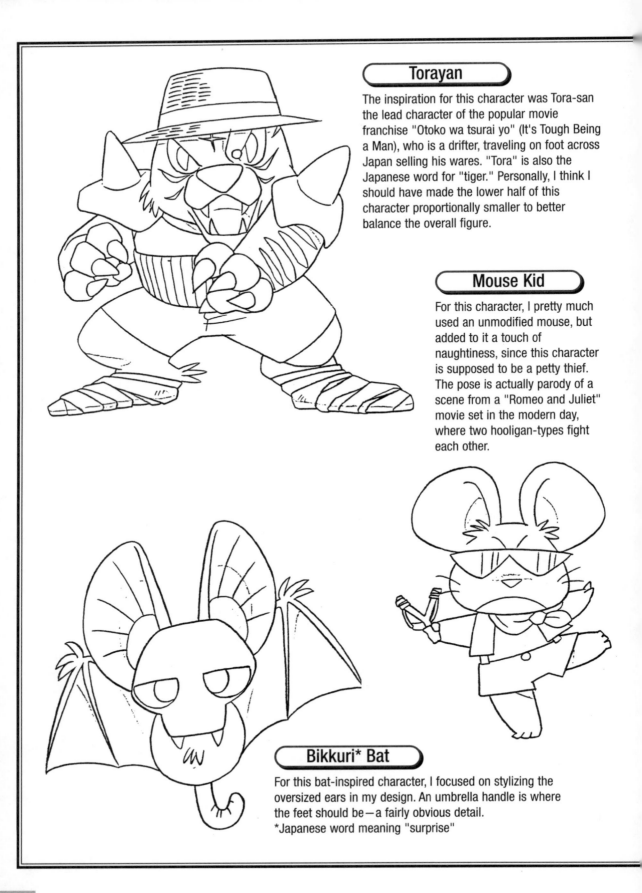

Torayan

The inspiration for this character was Tora-san the lead character of the popular movie franchise "Otoko wa tsurai yo" (It's Tough Being a Man), who is a drifter, traveling on foot across Japan selling his wares. "Tora" is also the Japanese word for "tiger." Personally, I think I should have made the lower half of this character proportionally smaller to better balance the overall figure.

Mouse Kid

For this character, I pretty much used an unmodified mouse, but added to it a touch of naughtiness, since this character is supposed to be a petty thief. The pose is actually parody of a scene from a "Romeo and Juliet" movie set in the modern day, where two hooligan-types fight each other.

Bikkuri* Bat

For this bat-inspired character, I focused on stylizing the oversized ears in my design. An umbrella handle is where the feet should be—a fairly obvious detail.
*Japanese word meaning "surprise"

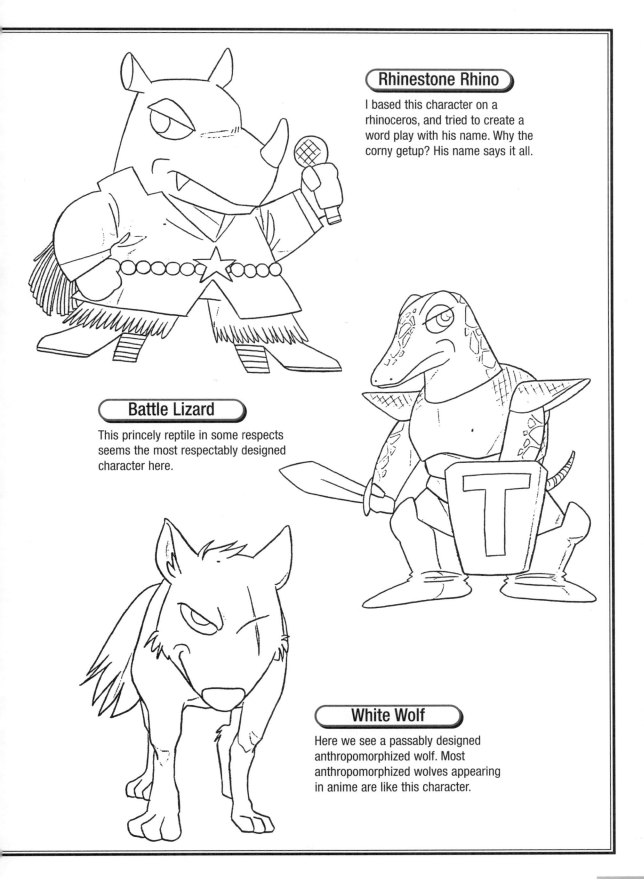

Rhinestone Rhino

I based this character on a rhinoceros, and tried to create a word play with his name. Why the corny getup? His name says it all.

Battle Lizard

This princely reptile in some respects seems the most respectably designed character here.

White Wolf

Here we see a passably designed anthropomorphized wolf. Most anthropomorphized wolves appearing in anime are like this character.

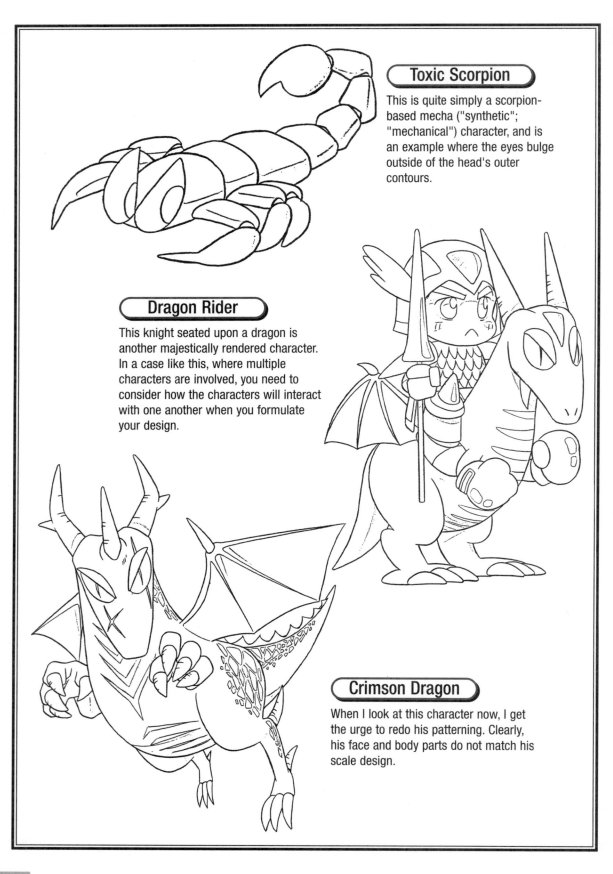

Toxic Scorpion

This is quite simply a scorpion-based mecha ("synthetic"; "mechanical") character, and is an example where the eyes bulge outside of the head's outer contours.

Dragon Rider

This knight seated upon a dragon is another majestically rendered character. In a case like this, where multiple characters are involved, you need to consider how the characters will interact with one another when you formulate your design.

Crimson Dragon

When I look at this character now, I get the urge to redo his patterning. Clearly, his face and body parts do not match his scale design.

Chapter 3
Things Can Be Chibis Too!

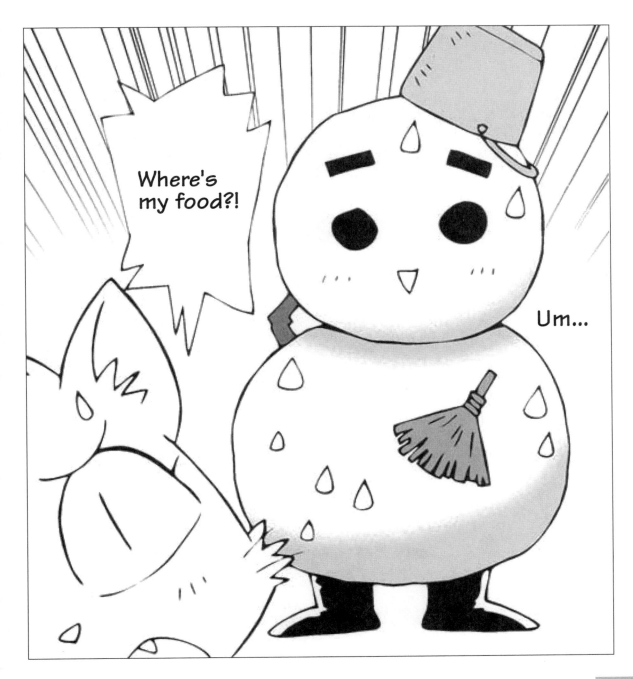

Ultra-Stylized Objects

Up to now we have primarily discussed the stylization of animals or creatures that feel emotions to a certain extent. However, in this chapter, we cover the ultra-stylization of inanimate objects that feel no emotions and have no will of their own. We also discuss techniques for giving these objects the illusion of will.

How many of the readers have seen animated movies in which appear lamps that talk and teapots that laugh and cry? I suspect quite a number of you have. This chapter presents techniques for portraying as inanimate objects with no emotions or free will of their own living, breathing beings. We begin by discussing simultaneously how to turn an object into a chibi character and how to anthropomorphize inanimate objects. You may find the discussion a bit difficult to follow, but hang in there. It'll be worth the effort.

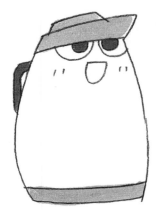

Anthropomorphization Key Point
A chief aspect of inanimate objects is that they cannot move. Consequently, you will need to decide whether you will enable such a character to move, or whether it will remain fixed in place when it plays its role.

Anthropomorphization Key Point
If the character must be shown in motion, then you need to visualize the character as a human and determine which parts of the inanimate object should be designed to correspond to human body parts.

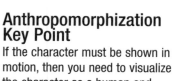

Sniffle Sniffle

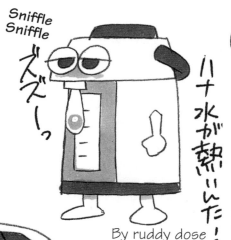

By ruddy dose ! burns!

Anthropomorphization Key Point
Since chairs have "legs" anyway, they become interchangeable with human legs. But, what about the hands? You should consider these points and construct your design so that a third person could look at the character and recognize the various corresponding parts.

Hehehehehe

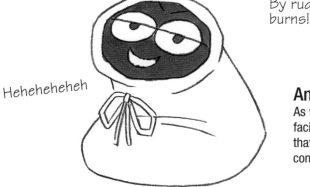

Anthropomorphization Key Point
As we have been discussing throughout this book, facial expressions may be easily portrayed provided that the face is well proportioned. As the artist, consider carefully where to position the face.

Anthropomorphized Family in Four Panels

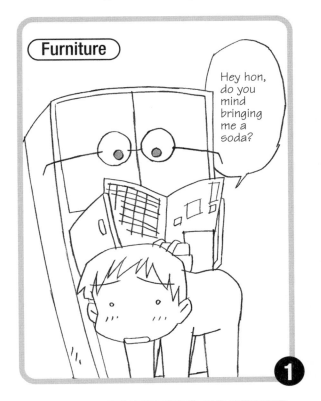

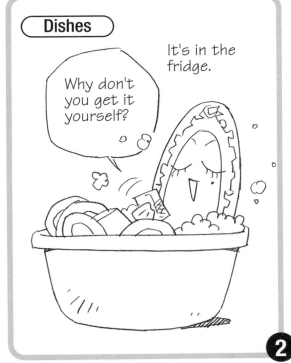

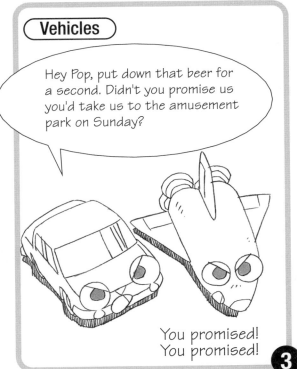

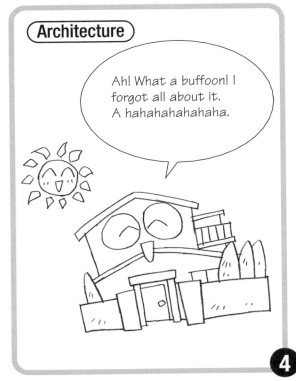

Yet another peaceful day.

Bowls and TV Sets

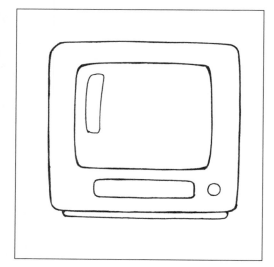

Realistic Rendition

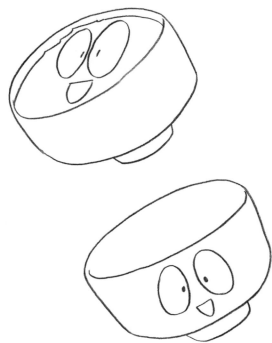

Anthropomorphized Character

Anthropomorphized Character

Take a gander at my antenna. They don't make indoor antennas like this anymore. (Most likely, anyway.)

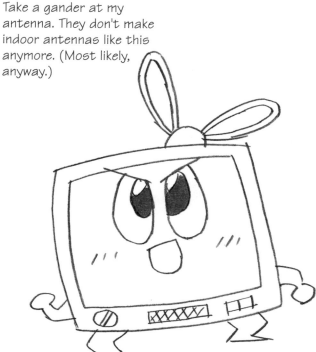

Unlike chairs, it is relatively easy to decide where to position the face on a TV set. But, what should you do about the arms and legs? Old-fashioned TV sets came with legs, so that would not be an issue. However, since now TVs rarely have legs, you might as well tack on a pair. You really have no alternative. Now then, if you plan to add arms and legs to a TV, you will need to ensure, just as you would with a human character, that the legs are positioned such that the figure is balanced in terms of its center of gravity. The issue of where to place the arms, on the other hand, perhaps has more to do with aesthetics. Most commonly, the arms are positioned on a level somewhere beneath the eyes. Even though this is a stylized character, placing the arms above the face will could it appear more like a bizarre monstrosity than a chibi inanimate object. While this may not always be the case, it is still probably a good idea to remember this point.

Knives and Drums

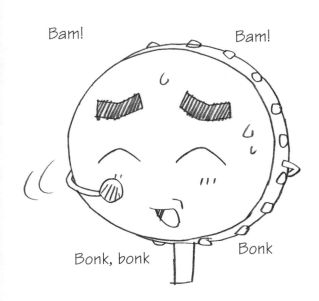

Realistic Rendition

Anthropomorphized Character

When people talk about razor-sharp guys, they mean gentlemen such as ourselves.

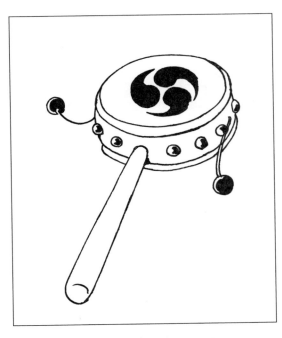

Bam!

Bam!

Bonk, bonk

Bonk

Anthropomorphized Character

Realistic Rendition

119

Buckets and Mechanical Pencils

Occasionally when having an inanimate object character perform a role, artists encounter difficulties adding arms and legs, or when they do, they find the overall look of the character is dramatically affected. Another option that must be considered in such cases is having the character perform without arms and legs. Imagine the character is an animate, living creature with the capacity to adapt and react, like the bucket you see below. There is an abundance of methods for suggesting movement that do not require the use of arms and legs. I also recommend studying modes of locomotion in insects.

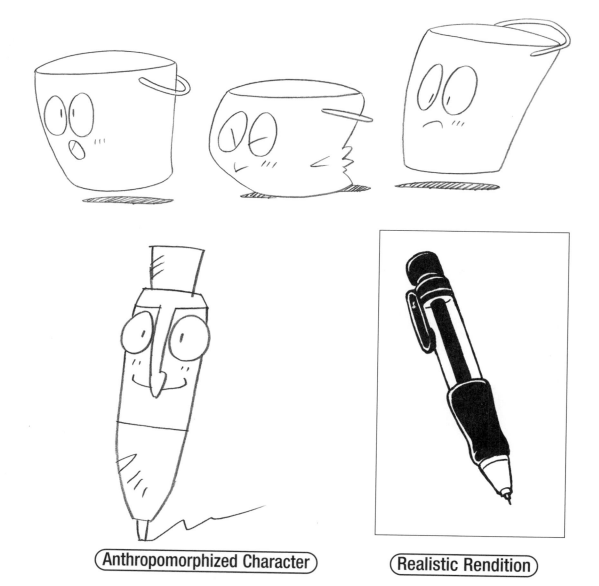

Anthropomorphized Character

Anthropomorphized Character

Realistic Rendition

Irons and Geta (Platform shoe on two wooden slats and a wooden base for the sole with a thong dividing the toes)

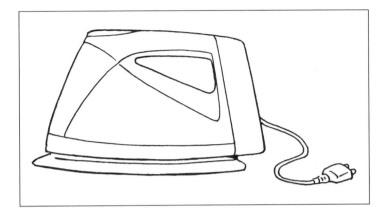

(Realistic Rendition)

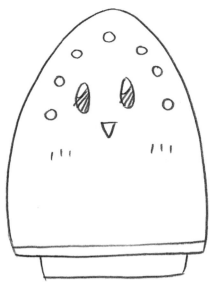

As mentioned previously, when giving an inanimate object a face, you will encounter the issue of where to position the face. The character can project diametrically opposite personalities depending on where its face is positioned, such as illustrated in the two geta characters below. Again, there is no correct answer in this matter, so try a variety of positions and select the placement you feel best suits the role you wish your character to play.

(Anthropomorphized Character)

(Anthropomorphized Character)

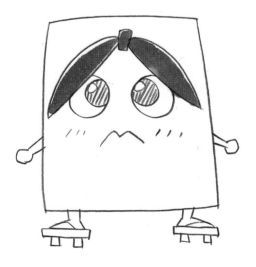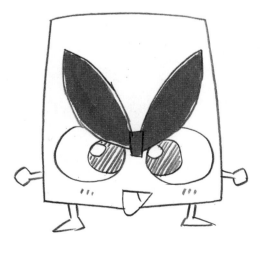

Fans and Brushes

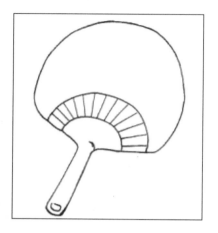

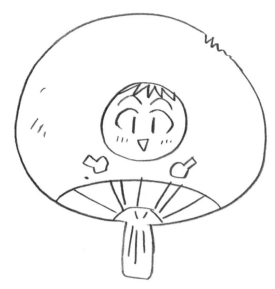

Anthropomorphized Character

Realistic Rendition

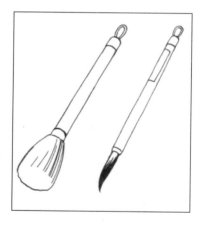

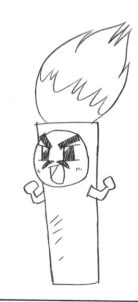

Anthropomorphized Character

For anthropomorphized characters, an option is
to add a face as if it were a person wearing
a costume. However, this style will have the
effect of making the viewer feel he or she is
watching a costume performance, so use the
method you feel best matches the intended role.

Batteries, Lipstick, and Balloons

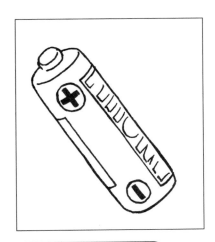

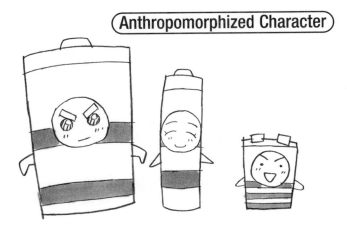

Anthropomorphized Character

Realistic Rendition

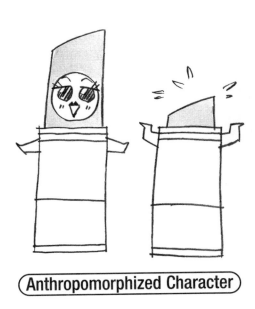

Anthropomorphized Character

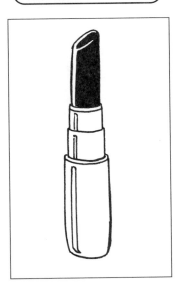

Things come in various categories and diverse forms. Exploit these different forms when you design your character. Provided that the viewer is able to recognize what object the character represents, skillful use of the various forms will help you sculpt the character's individuality.

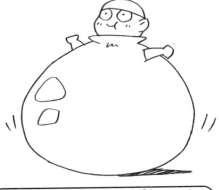

Anthropomorphized Character

Dishes and Newspapers

Some objects change their forms, and depending on where you elect to locate the face, the face may become obscured when the object's form changes. For example, if you were to anthropomorphize a book and placed the face inside the book, then the face would be hidden from view when the book was closed. On the other hand, if you were to position the face on the book's front cover, then the face would disappear when the book was open. Consider how the character must play its role for a given scene when determining the face's placement.

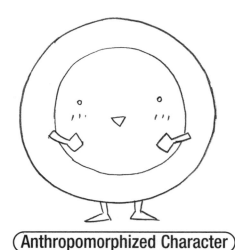

(Anthropomorphized Character)

(Realistic Rendition)

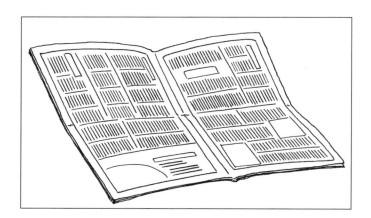

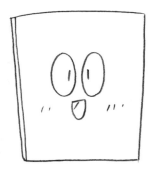  

(Anthropomorphized Character)

Couches and Soap

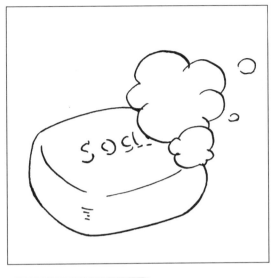

Realistic Rendition

Anthropomorphized Character

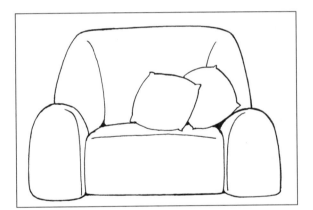

Realistic Rendition

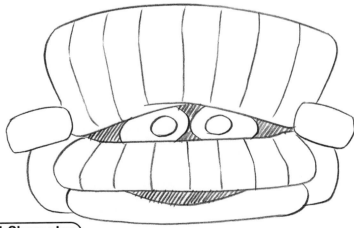

Anthropomorphized Character

Afterword

How did you enjoy "Volume 2: Animals"? There is a wealth of animals and objects we did not have space to cover in this book, so I recommend that you study those animals and objects near you and practice turning them into chibi characters.

As also mentioned in "Volume 1: Humans", regardless of whether your subject is an animal or an object, you will not be able to transform it successfully into a chibi character unless you have a firm grasp of its natural form. How does the animal move? How does it express itself? How is the object constructed? How is the object used? If you cannot answer these questions, then, as a creator, you will not be able to draw or bring your chibi characters to life.

Looking solely at the surface and failing to gain a deeper understanding will result in nothing more than a flimsy, short-lived illustration.

Please, as an artist, give the characters that you draw and bring to life a full-fledged world in which to live. They will respond favorably.

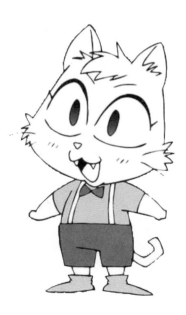

Artist Profile: Gen Sato

After joining Sunrise, Gen Sato later apprenticed under Yoshikazu Yasuhiko and joined Yasuhiko's studio. Sato produced his Gundam parody work, *Bakusho Senshi SD Gundam* ["Riotously Funny Warrior SD Gundam"] published by Kodansha, and developing chibi characters as a distinct category. Sato is currently active as an anime and manga creator as well as instructs new generations of artists at various trade schools.

Anime Projects Participated

Ojamajo Doremi Dokkaan! [literally "Pestering Witch, Kaboom!"], *Ashita no Naaja* [literally "Tomorrow's Nadja"], *Futari wa Purikyua* [literally "The Pretty Cure Pair", *Ippatsu Kanta-kun* [literally "One-hit Kanta"], *Shin Lupin Sansei* [literally "New Lupin III"], *Sutajingaa* [English title "Spaceketeers"], *Gatchaman II*, *Pinkuredy Monogatari* [literally "Pink Ladies' Story"], *Ashita no Joe II* [literally "Tomorrow's Joe"], *Uchu Senkan Yamato II* [English title "Space Battleship Yamato II"], *Zendaman*, *Ginga Tetsudo 999* [English title "Galaxy Express 999"], *Uchu Senshi Baldios* [literally "Space Warrior Baldios"], *Sengoku Majin Goshogun* [literally "Goshogun, Demon of the Warring States"], *Daioja*, *Gundam II*, *Gundam III*, *Votoms*, *Crusher Joe*, *Kyojin Gogu* [literally "Titan Gogu"], *Dirty Pair*, *Futari Taka* [literally "Two Hawks"], *Maitchingu Machiko Sensei* [English title "Miss Machiko"], *Manga Hajimete Monogatari* [literally "First-Time-in-Manga Stories"], *SD Gundam I to VI*, and others.

Single Volume Comics

Oyasumi! Watashi no Saiboi [literally "Goodnight, My Cyborg Boy"]: Tokuma Shoten Publishing Co., Ltd.
Aidoru Tantei Hiroshi ni Omakase [literally "Leave it to Hiroshi, Dashing Detective"]: Tokuma Shoten Publishing Co., Ltd.
Famikon Hissho Dojo [literally "Family Computer, Go Ahead and Laugh"] (3-volume series): Kodansha Ltd.
Bakusho Senshi SD Gundam ["Riotously Funny Warrior SD Gundam"] (8-volume series): Kodansha Ltd.
Mina-san! Banbaman desu yo!! ["Everyone! It's Bomberman!!"] (4-volume series): Kodansha Ltd.
Binpatsu Ichiban [roughly "Best in Hair"] (2-volume series): Kadokawa Shoten Publishing Co., Ltd.
Famikon Tanteidan [literally "Family Computer Detective Squad"] (2-volume series): Akita Publishing Co., Ltd.
and others.

Misc.

Nippen no Miko-chan (3rd generation of the commercial manga character),
Movie: Tokiwa-so no Seishun ["Tokiwa: The Manga Apartment"] (as Manga Production Supervisor),
Nippon Television FAN (as Program Illustrator, etc.),
and others.

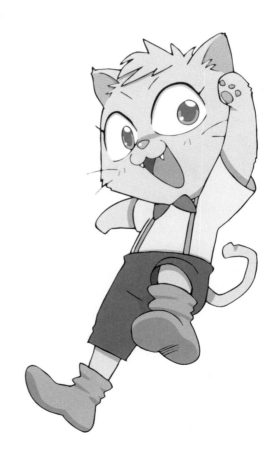